⊢ COLORING ⊣

LIZARDS, SNAKES, & MORE

SOUTHERN CALIFORNIA

Bradford D. Hollingsworth

Special Thanks to our Sponsor

RANCHO LA PUERTA
Tecate · Baja California · Mexico

Sunbelt Publications, Inc.
Chula Vista, California

D1534353

Dr. Bradford Hollingsworth, Curator of Herpetology for the San Diego Natural History Museum, has had a life-long interest in the diversity of amphibians and reptiles. His research focuses on the systematics and biogeography of amphibians and reptiles of the Southwest, including the Baja California peninsula and its associated islands. He is responsible for the care and maintenance of Museum's 78,000 amphibian and reptile research specimens and regularly teaches as an adjunct professor at San Diego State University.

Additionally, Dr. Hollingsworth launched the *Amphibian and Reptile Atlas of Peninsular California*. The goal of the Atlas is to combine both Museum collection data and observations from citizen scientists to help better understand the biodiversity of our region. The Atlas is a binational effort spanning from southern California to the tip of Baja California.

Dr. Hollingsworth is donating his author royalties to the San Diego Natural History Museum.

Coloring Lizards, Snakes, & More: Southern California
Part of the *Color & Learn* Series

Sunbelt Publications, Inc.
Copyright © 2020 by Bradford D. Hollingsworth
All rights reserved. First edition 2020, second printing 2023

Cover and book design by Kristina Filley
Project management by Deborah Young

Printed in United States of America

Please direct comments and inquiries to:

664 Marsat Ct., Suite A
Chula Vista, CA 91911
(619) 258-4911, fax: (619) 258-4916
www.sunbeltpublications.com

26 25 24 23   5 4 3 2

All photographs are by the author unless noted.
Front cover: Zebra-tailed Lizard. Back cover Granite Spiny Lizard.

Introduction to *Coloring Lizards, Snakes, & More: Southern California*

Amphibians and reptiles have long fascinated nature lovers. With their great diversity of body forms and habits, they vary in how they move, communicate, feed, and reproduce. While some species have become adapted to our urban environments and are regularly seen in our back-yards, most require open space with intact natural landscapes and clean water. Many are nocturnal and active only at night, while others are masters of camouflage and remain hidden from view. Some are active only when it rains, while others require the heat of the hottest part of a summer day. Encountering them usually involves only a brief glimpse as they scurry to escape, so when the opportunity arises for more prolonged viewing, the encounter can bring heightened enjoyment as a small portion of their secretive lives is revealed.

The selection of illustrations in this coloring book is drawn from the San Diego Natural History Museum's *Amphibian and Reptile Atlas of Peninsular California* (herpatlas.sdnhm.org), which highlights the diversity of frogs, salamanders, turtles, snakes, and lizards from southern California and the Baja California peninsula. The Atlas includes over 180 species that live in this region. The amphibians and reptiles selected for this book provide a quick example of 40 different kinds of species that live in coastal and wetland areas, the foothill and mountains, and deserts of southern California.

Coloring amphibians and reptiles is a great way to prepare yourself for encountering these species in the field. Illustrations are often used in field guides because they call attention to key features that help identify an animal by focusing your attention on diagnostic characters or features unique to that species. And biologists have long used illustrations in their field notes to highlight their observations and note the features for the species they study.

The illustrations show the range of variation that amphibians and reptiles take on. Frogs are distinctive because they lack a tail as an adult, so their bodies have a compact center of gravity which aids them when they jump. Salamanders are amphibians that retain a tail and often have colorful markings to signal potential predators of powerful skin toxins. Turtles have shells to allow their head, neck, legs, and tail to be withdrawn to protect them from attack. Lizards are stunningly diverse with amazing characteristics. Some have horns and others display brightly colored markings. Their bodies are built to live in sand, trees, rocks, crevices, burrows, or flat on the ground. And snakes are limbless and use a wide-variety of hunting strategies including constriction and the use of lethal venoms.

The book is arranged with the coloring pages presented first with reference information in the back. The reference material includes a description of the species, photographs of each, and a checklist. The next step is to get outdoors and go on a hike. Bring a pair of binoculars and try to catch a glimpse of a lizard perched on a tree trunk or rock. With a little practice, you will be identifying many of the amphibians and reptiles that call southern California home.

The *Color & Learn* series of coloring books are designed to be informative. Enjoy coloring each image. The pages are printed one-sided on a heavy weight paper. Whatever medium is your preference, whether it be colored pencils, crayons, or pens, any of them can be used to color the illustrations. Once an image is completed, it can also be removed from the book to frame.

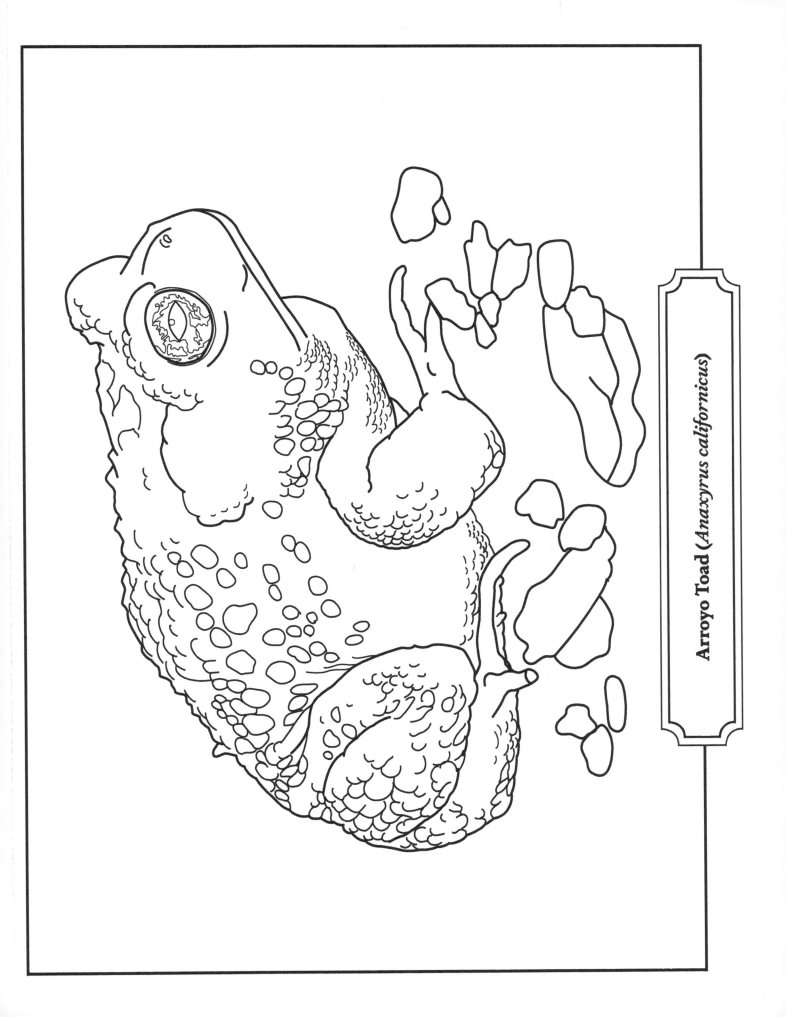

Arroyo Toad (*Anaxyrus californicus*)

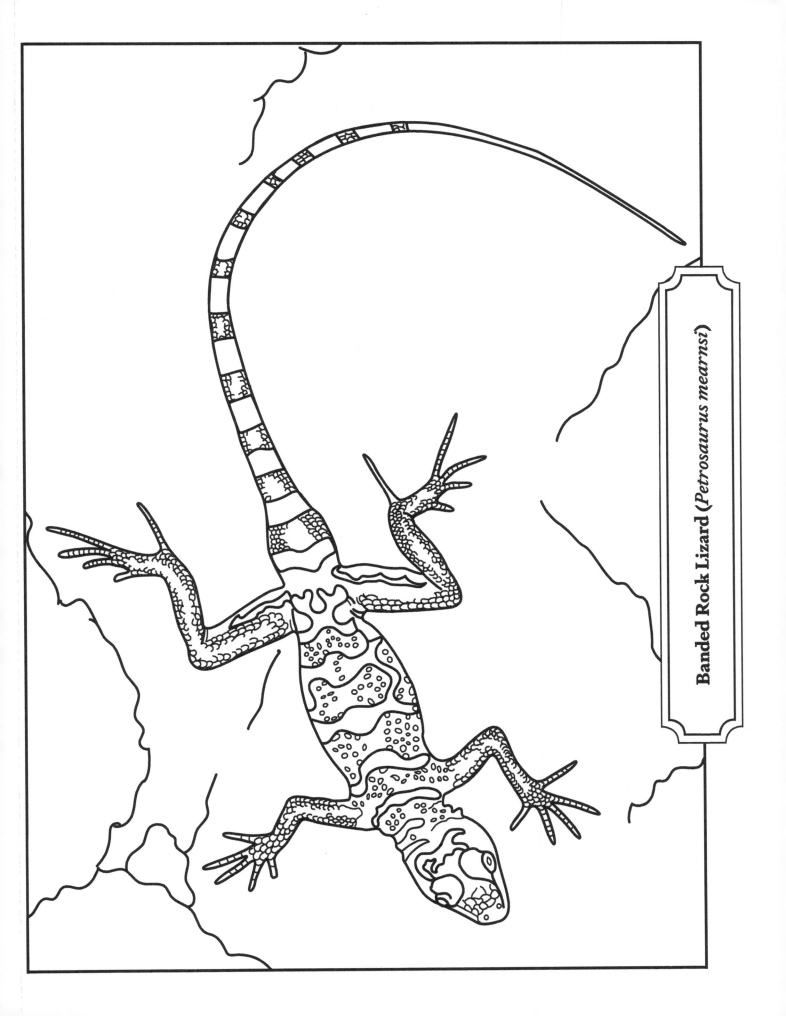

Banded Rock Lizard (*Petrosaurus mearnsi*)

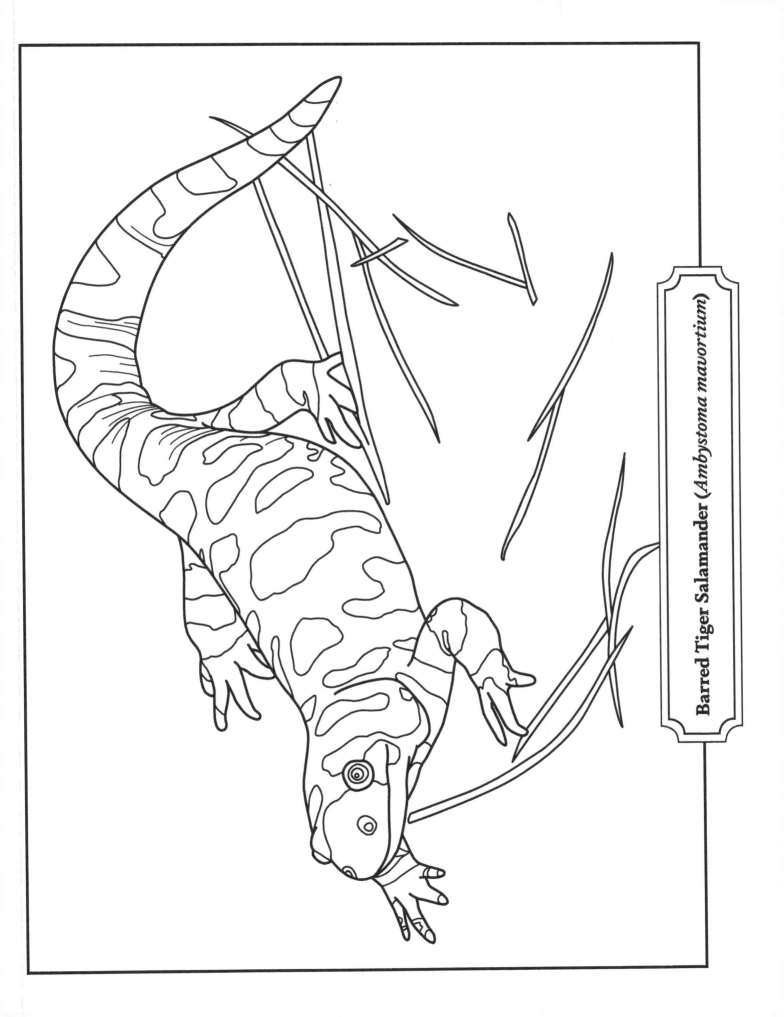

Barred Tiger Salamander (*Ambystoma mavortium*)

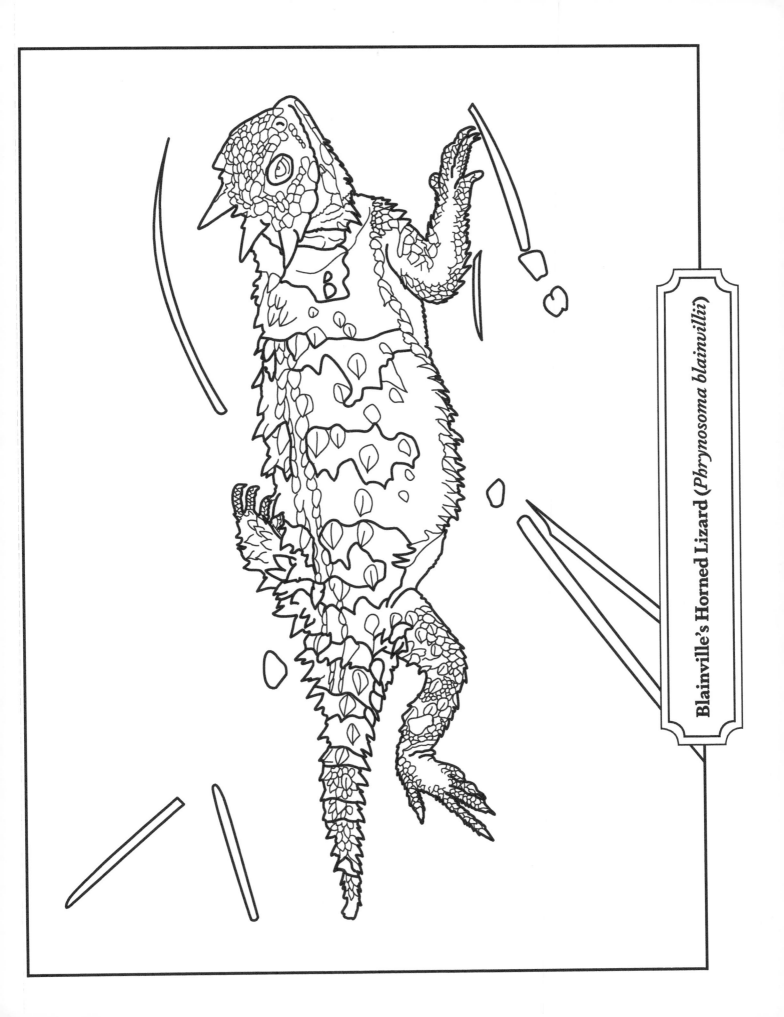

Blainville's Horned Lizard (*Phrynosoma blainvillii*)

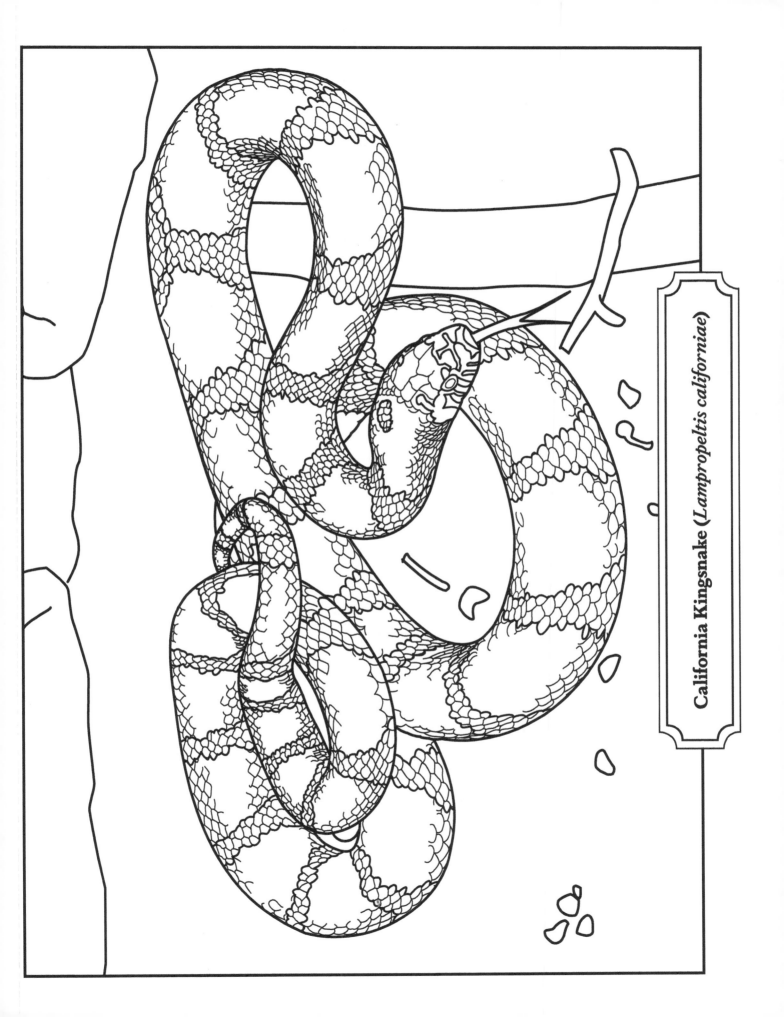

California Kingsnake (*Lampropeltis californiae*)

California Newt (*Taricha torosa*)

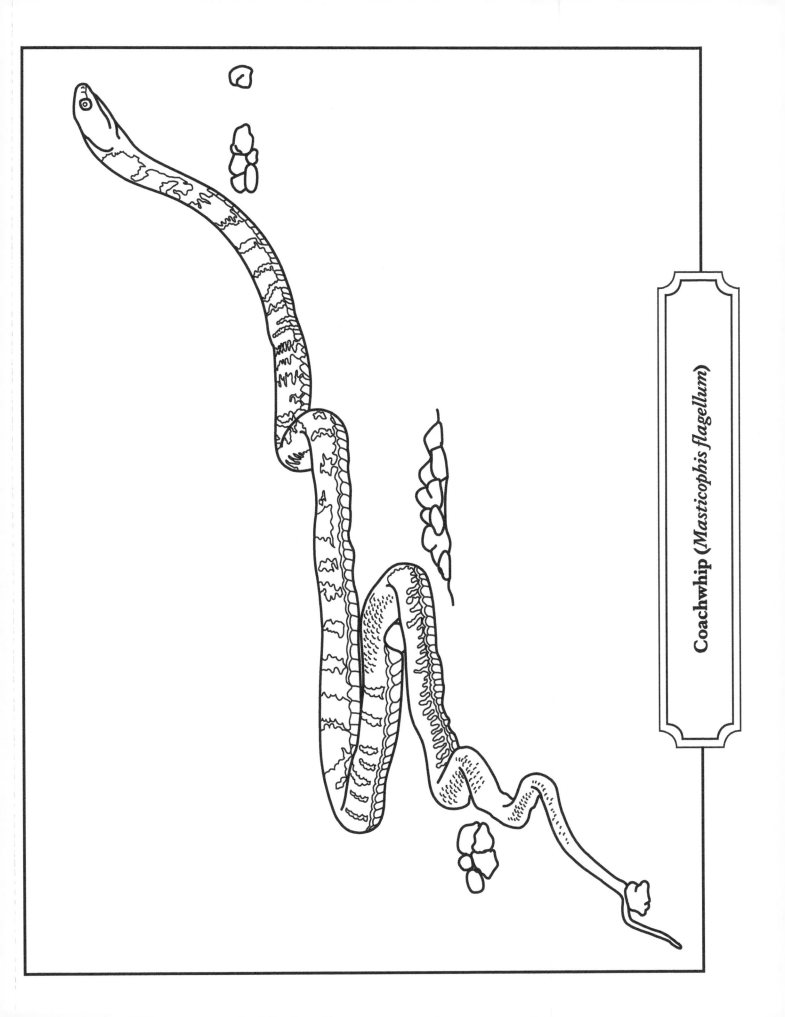

Coachwhip (*Masticophis flagellum*)

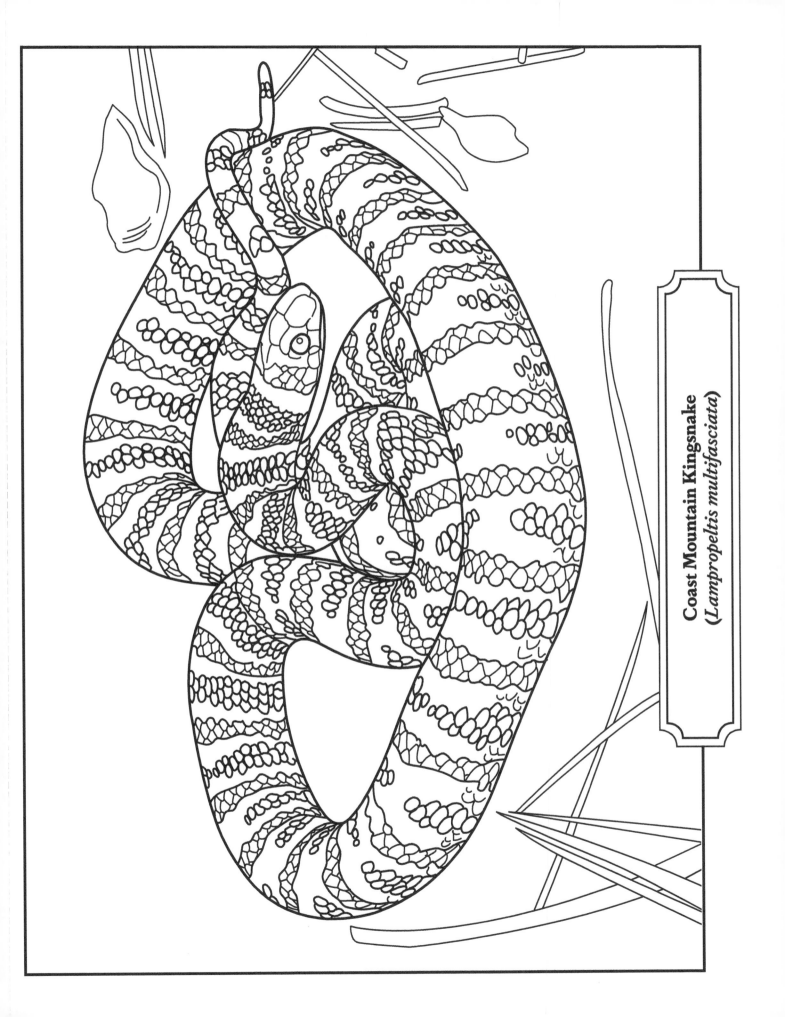

Coast Mountain Kingsnake
(*Lampropeltis multifasciata*)

Common Chuckwalla (*Sauromalus ater*)

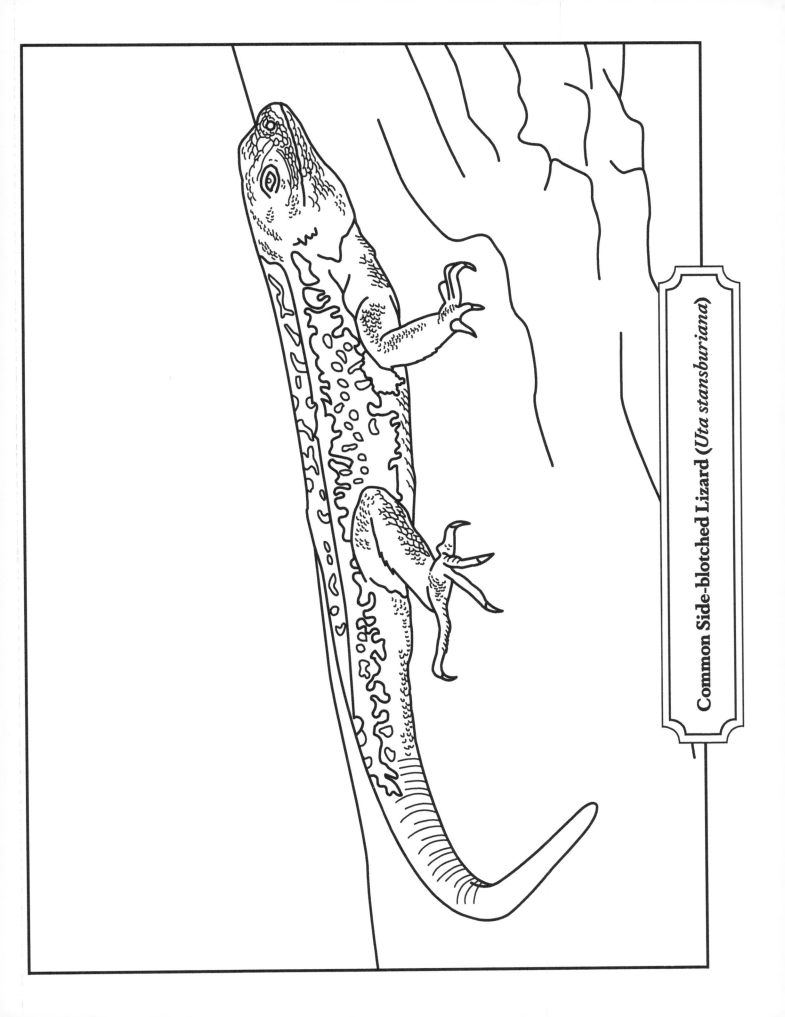

Common Side-blotched Lizard (*Uta stansburiana*)

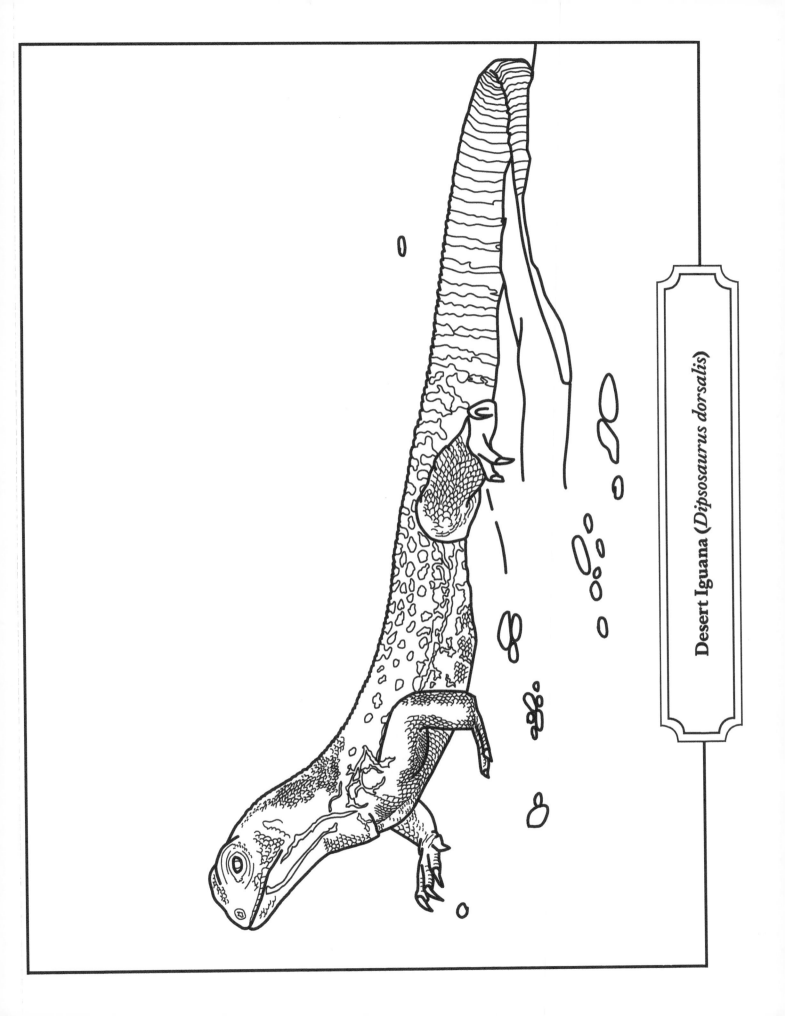

Desert Iguana (*Dipsosaurus dorsalis*)

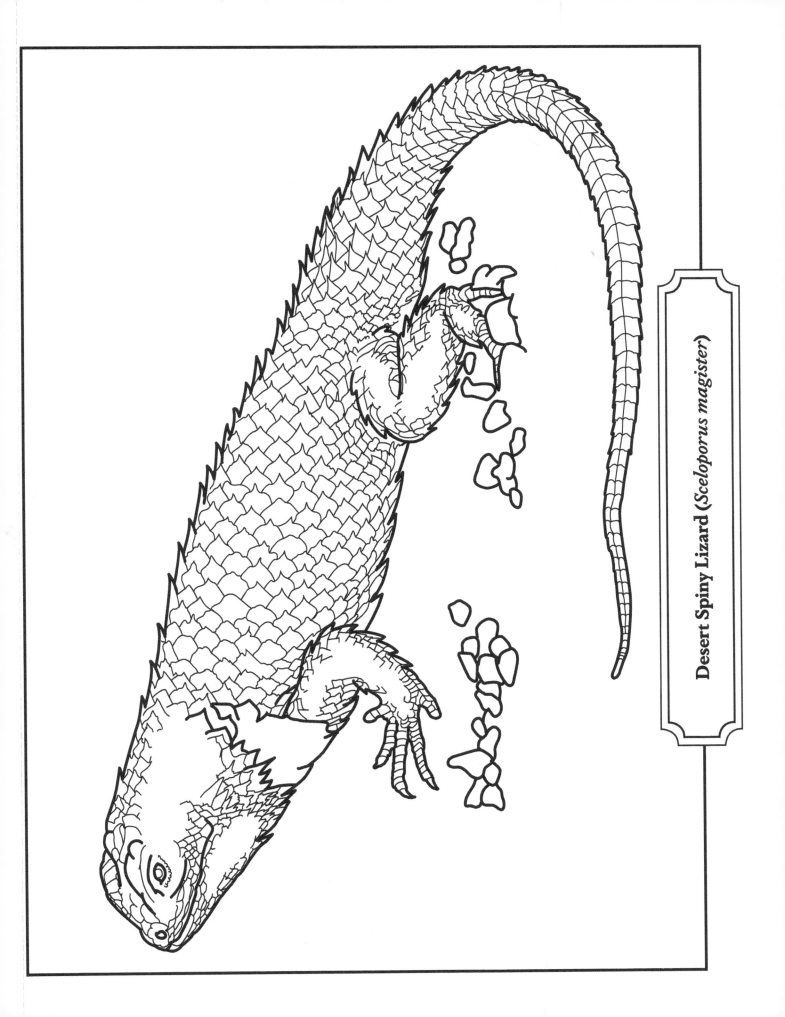

Desert Spiny Lizard (*Sceloporus magister*)

Desert Tortoise (*Gopherus agassizii*)

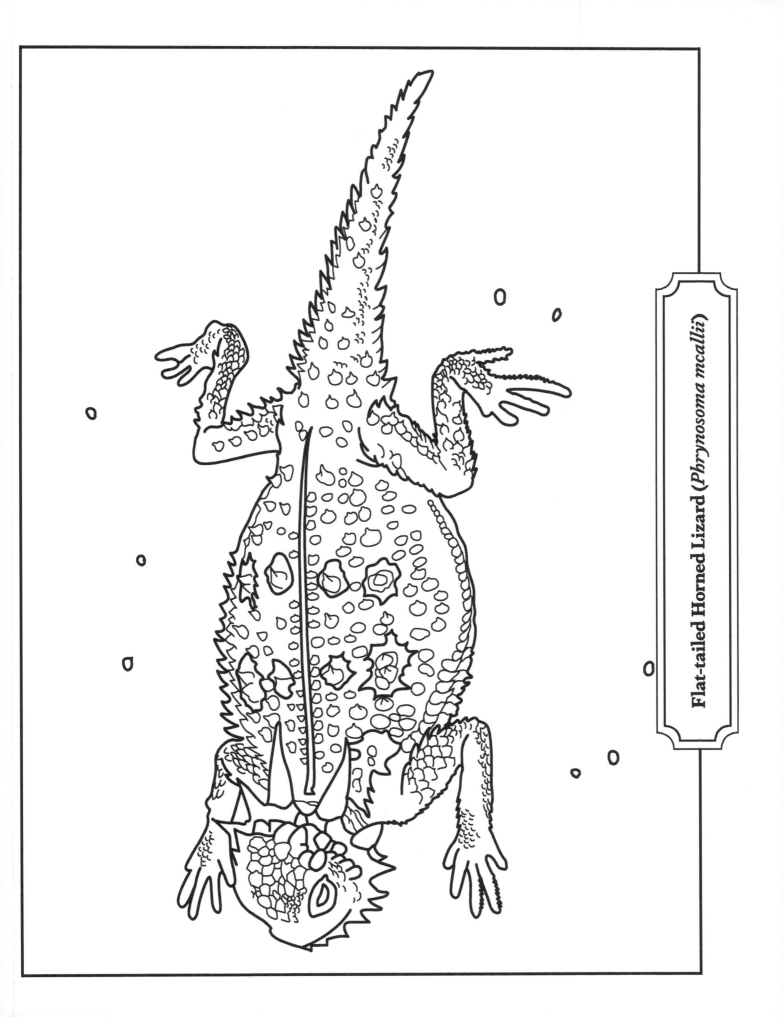

Flat-tailed Horned Lizard (*Phrynosoma mcallii*)

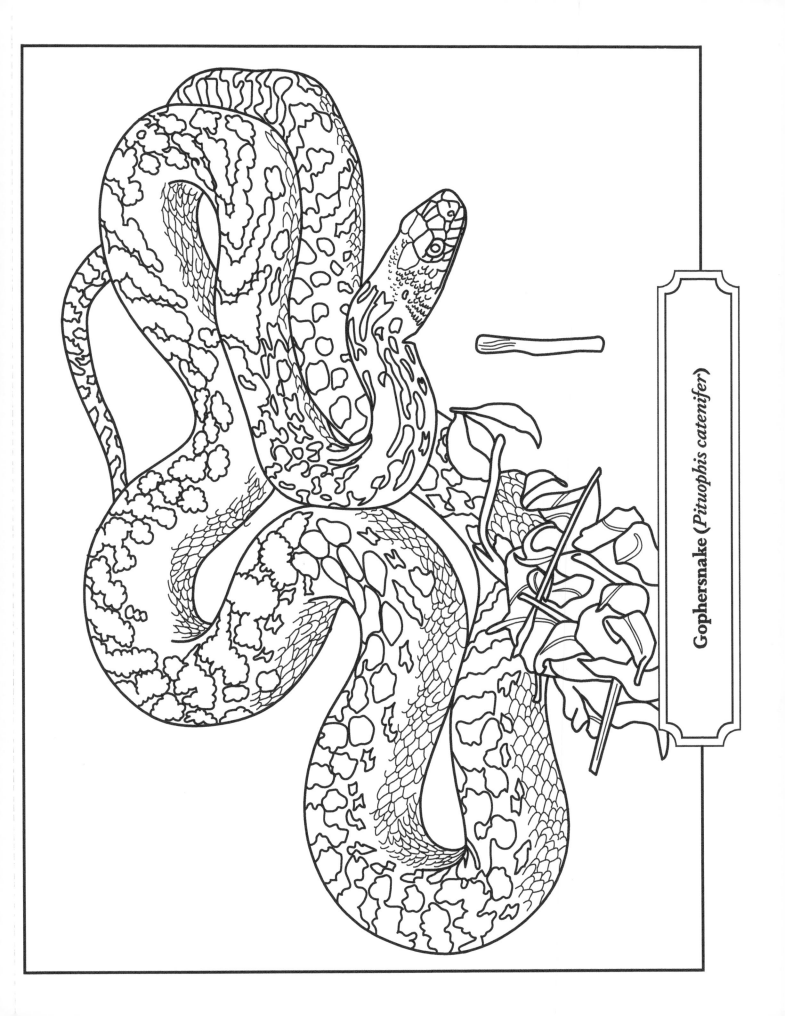

Gophersnake (*Pituophis catenifer*)

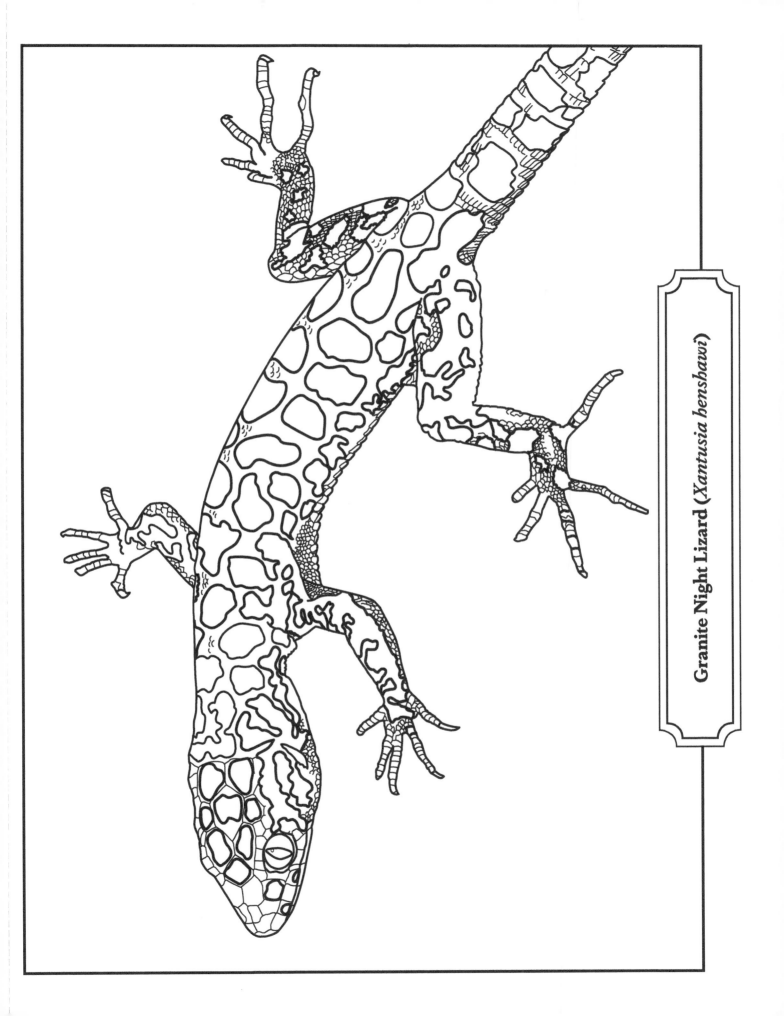

Granite Night Lizard (*Xantusia henshawi*)

Granite Spiny Lizard (*Sceloporus orcutti*)

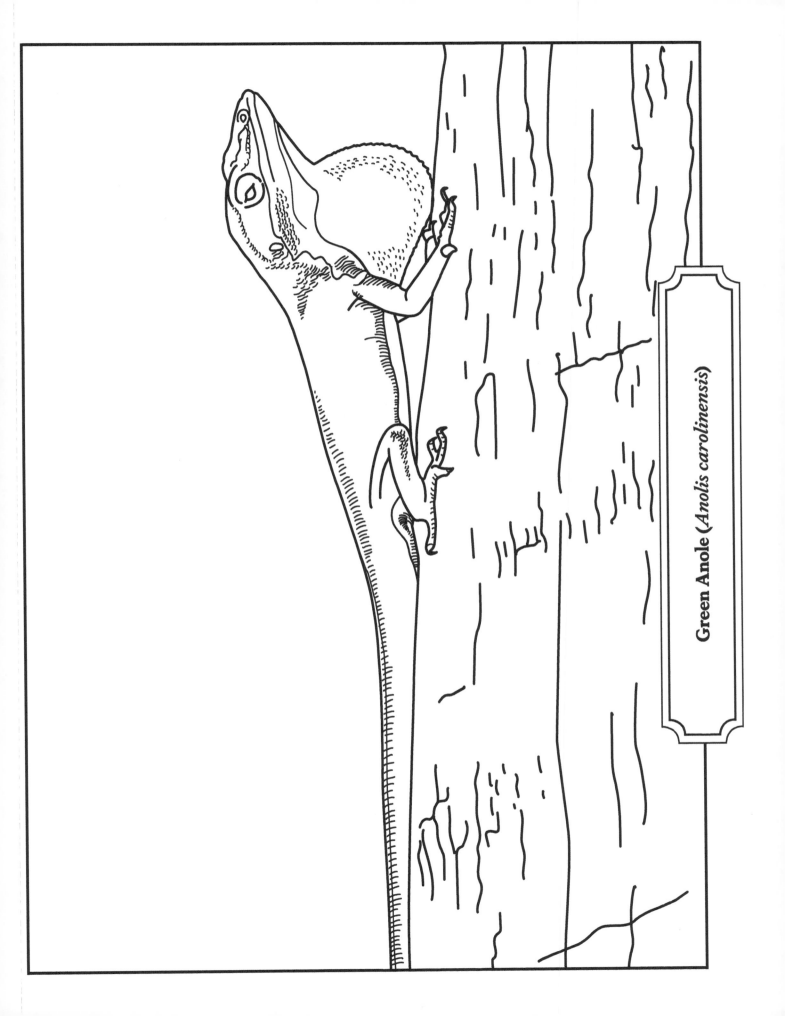

Green Anole (*Anolis carolinensis*)

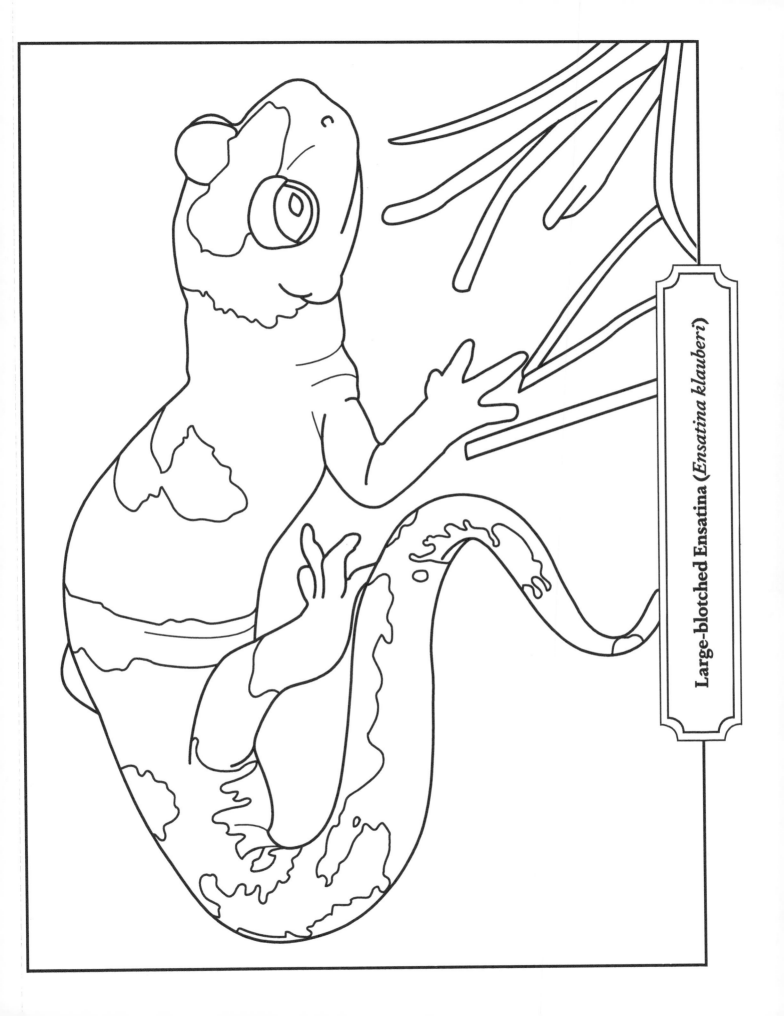

Large-blotched Ensatina (*Ensatina klauberi*)

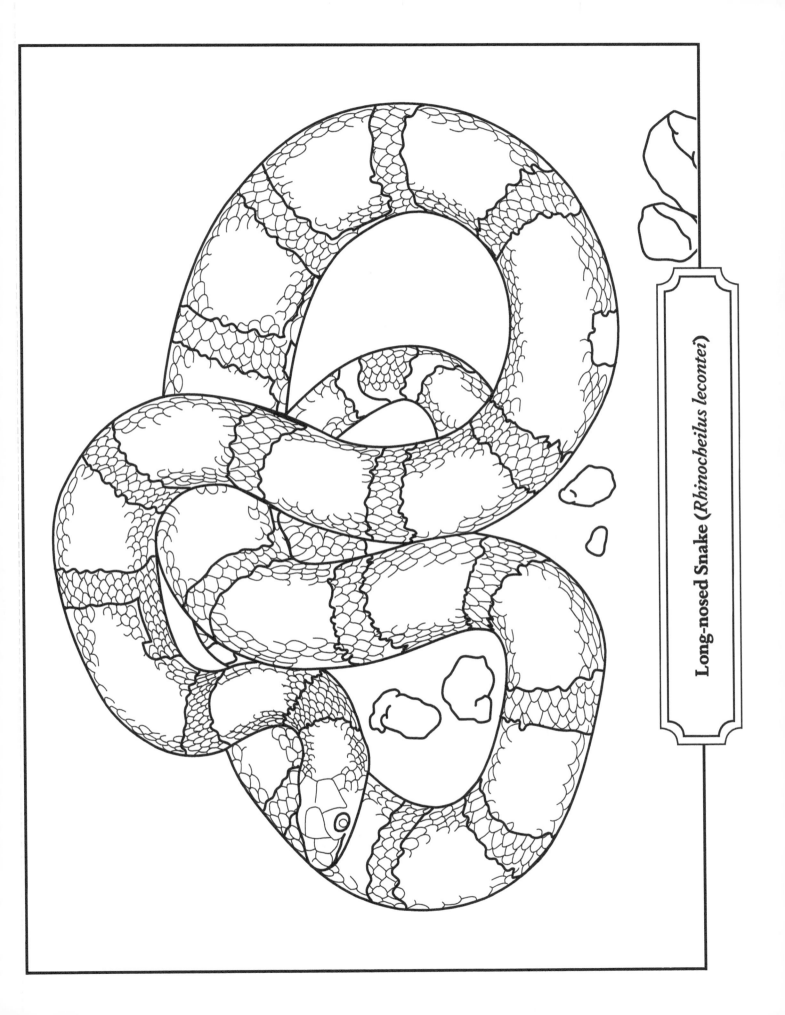

Long-nosed Snake (*Rhinocheilus lecontei*)

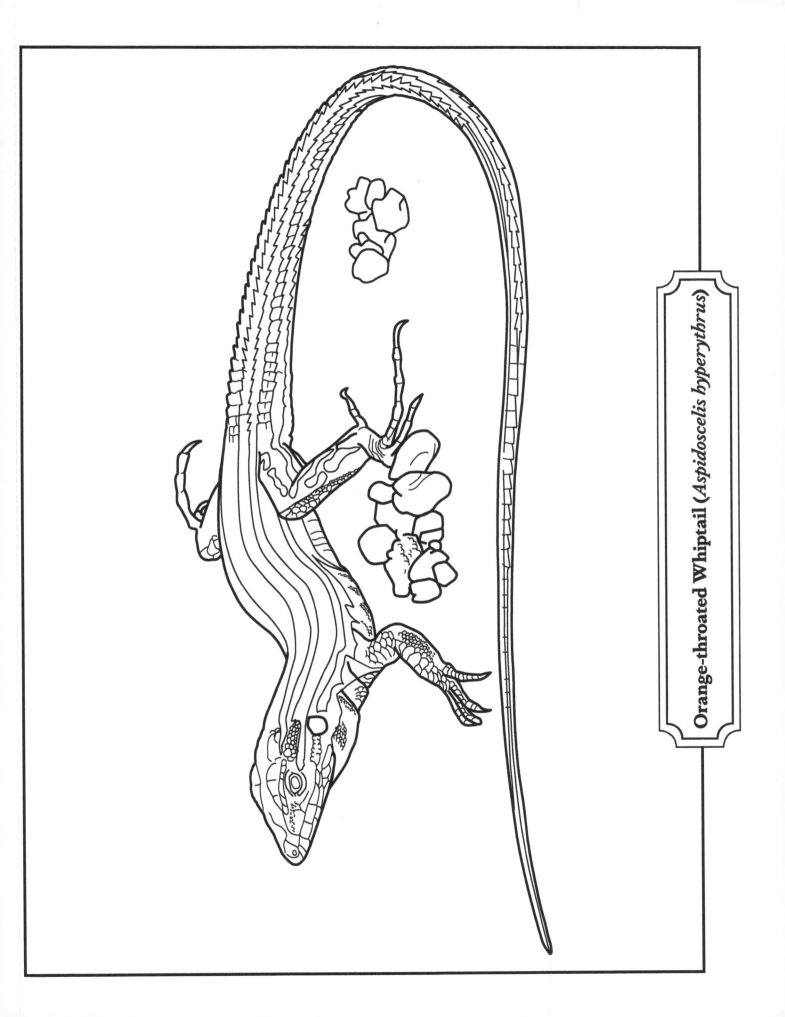

Orange-throated Whiptail (*Aspidoscelis hyperythrus*)

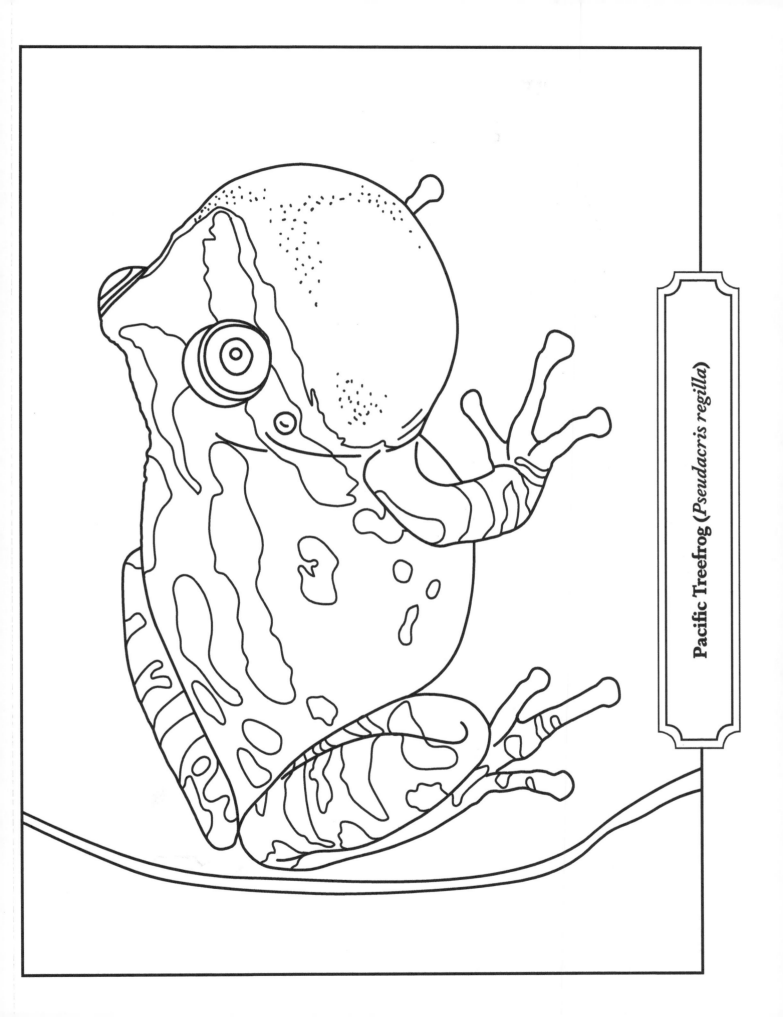

Pacific Treefrog (*Pseudacris regilla*)

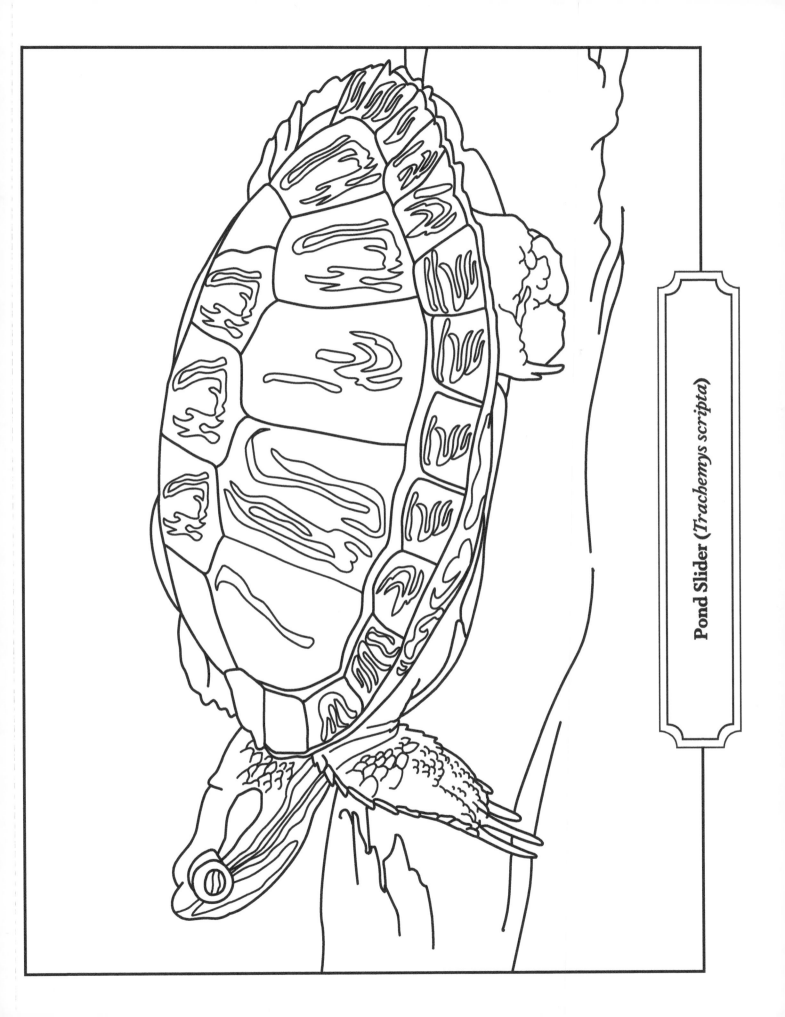

Pond Slider (*Trachemys scripta*)

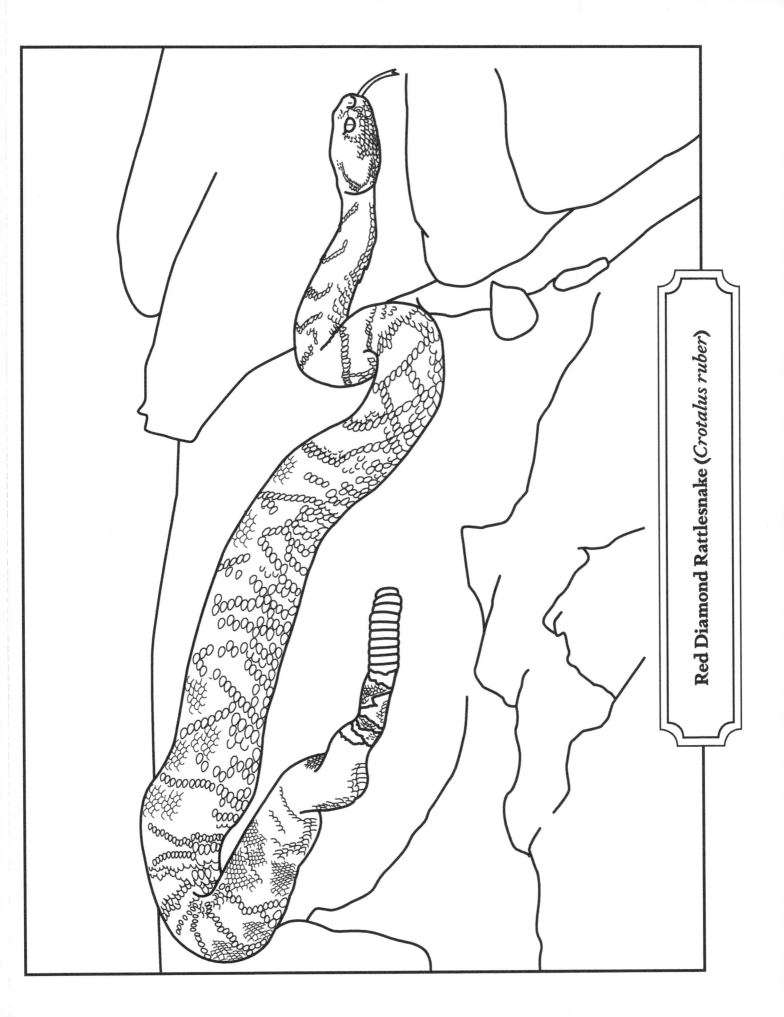

Red Diamond Rattlesnake (*Crotalus ruber*)

Red-spotted Toad (*Anaxyrus punctatus*)

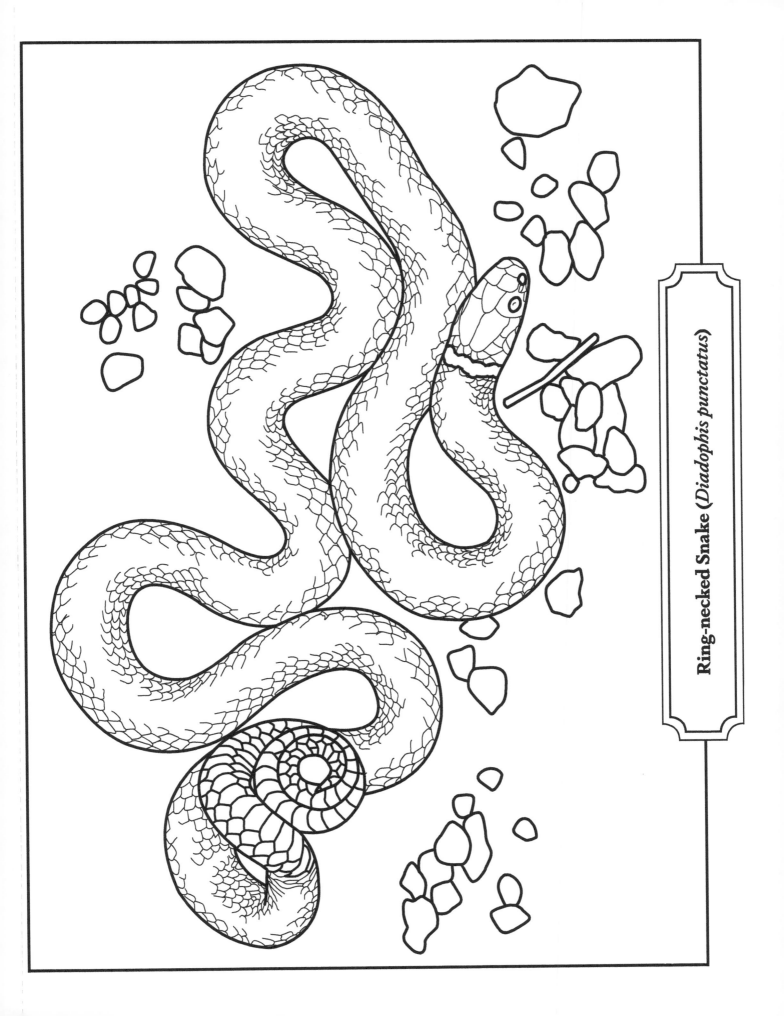

Ring-necked Snake (*Diadophis punctatus*)

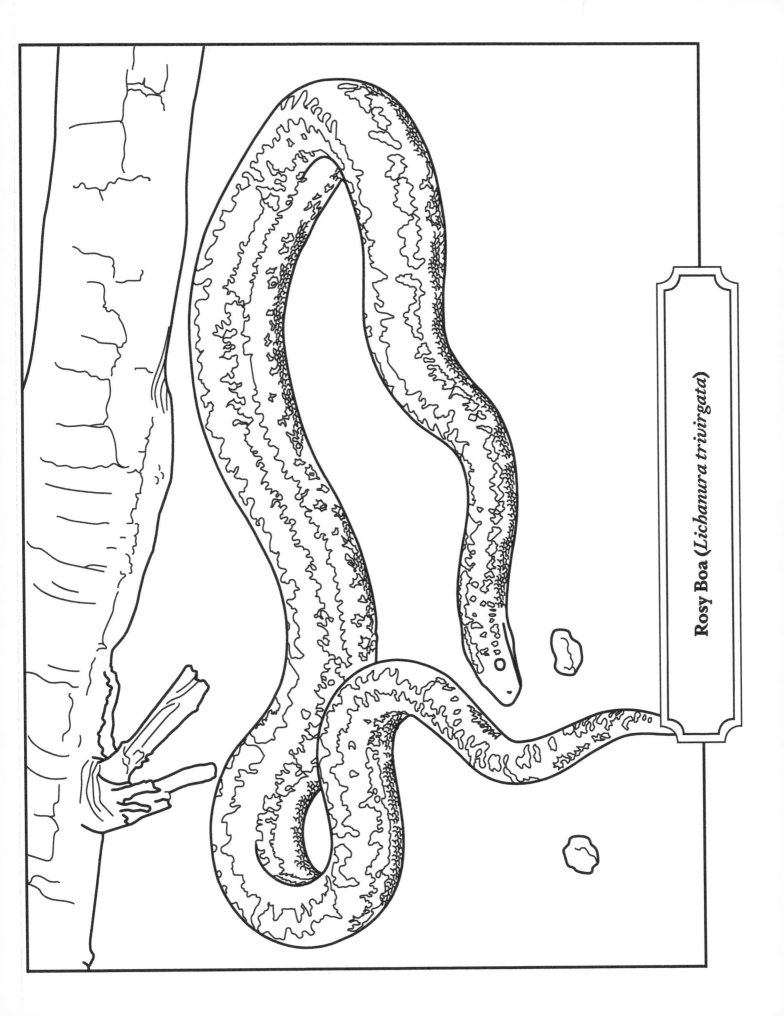

Rosy Boa (*Lichanura trivirgata*)

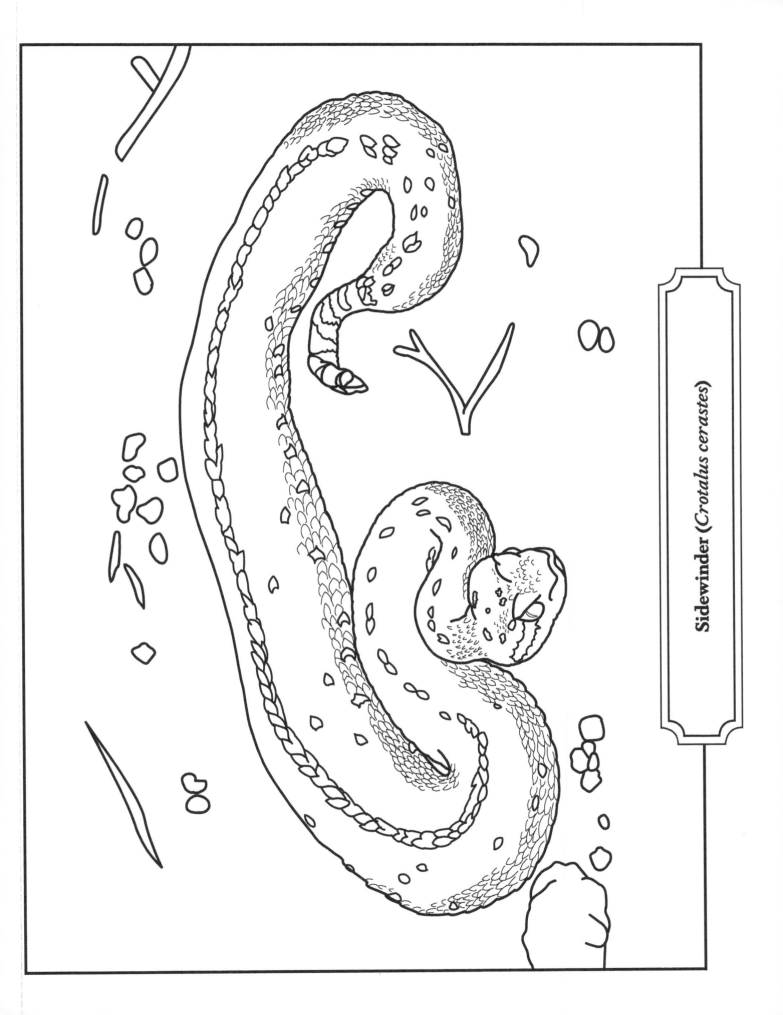

Sidewinder (*Crotalus cerastes*)

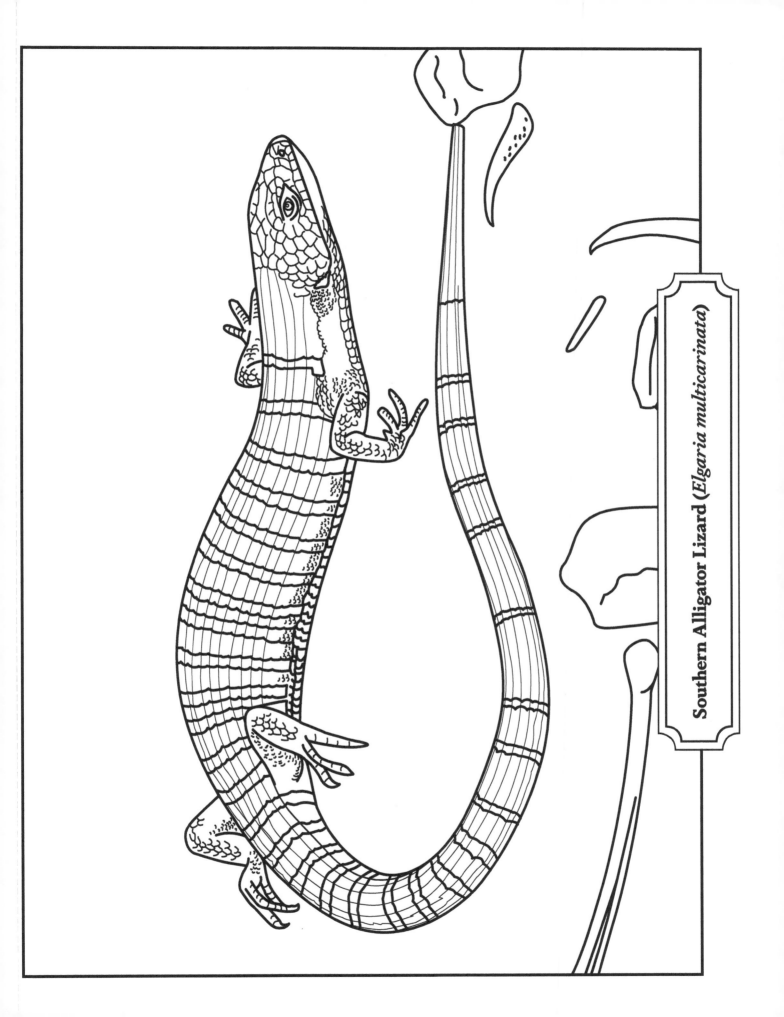

Southern Alligator Lizard (*Elgaria multicarinata*)

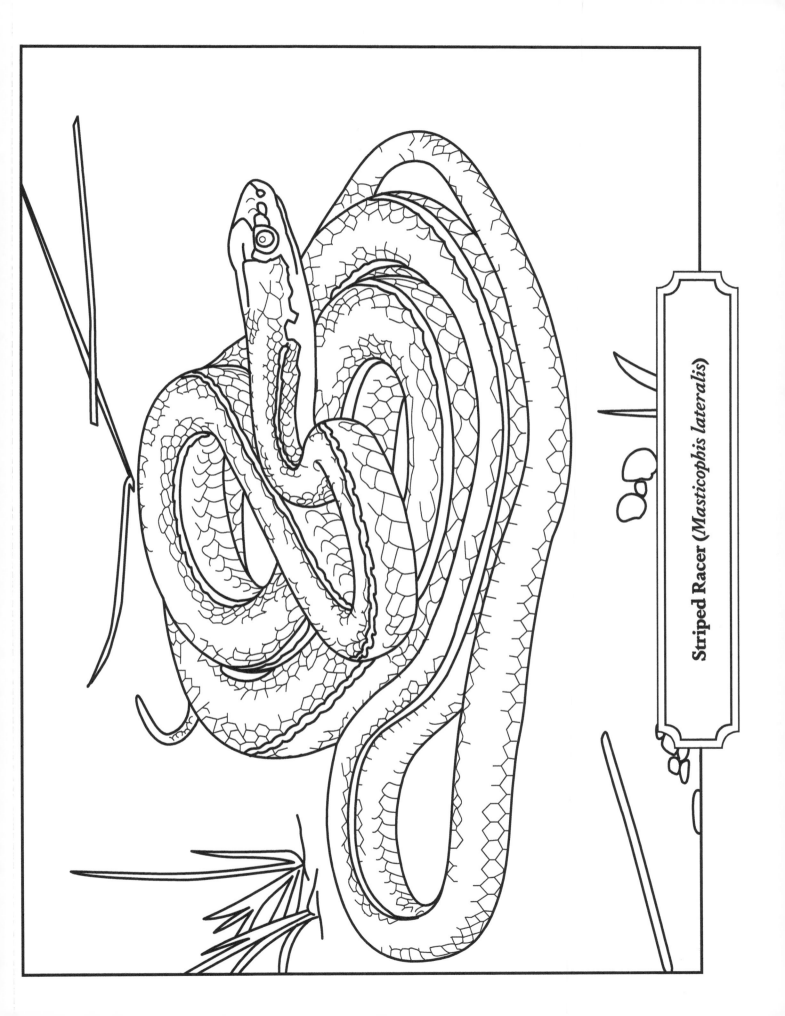

Striped Racer (*Masticophis lateralis*)

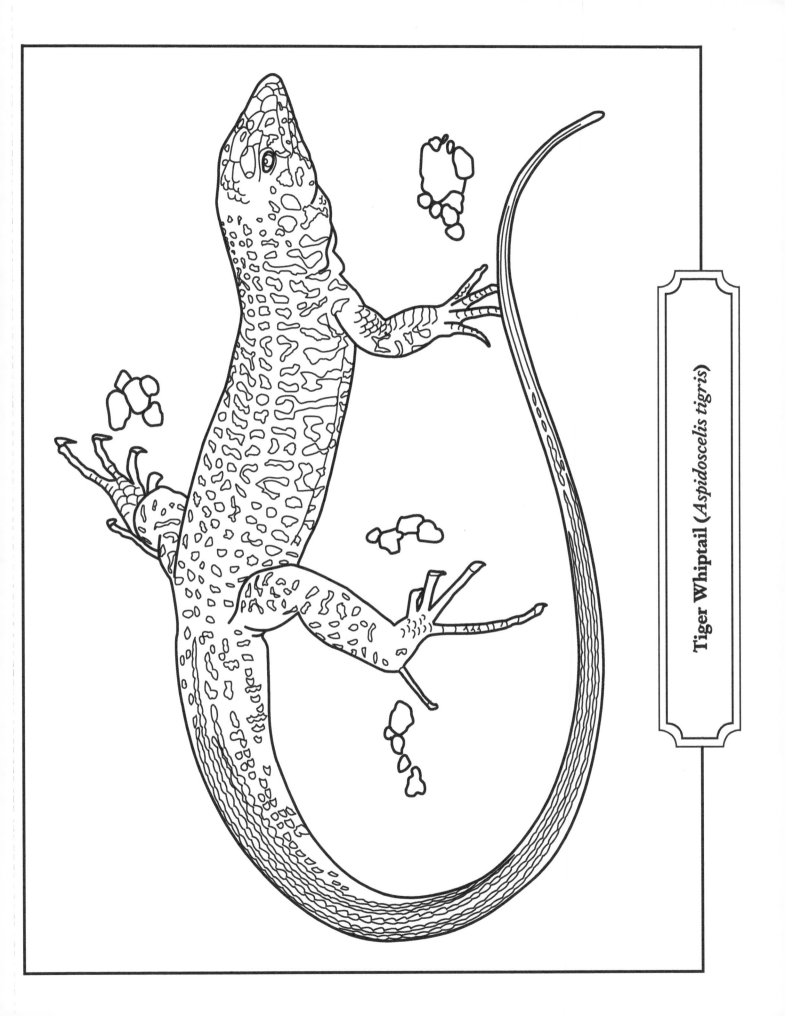

Tiger Whiptail (*Aspidoscelis tigris*)

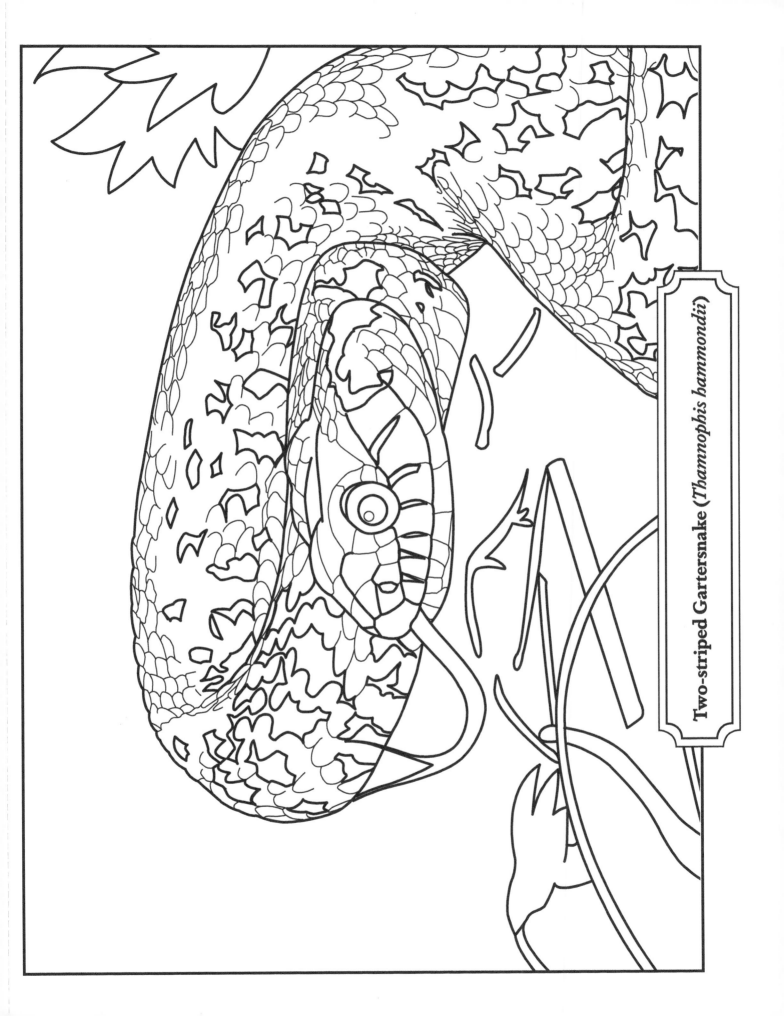

Two-striped Gartersnake (*Thamnophis hammondii*)

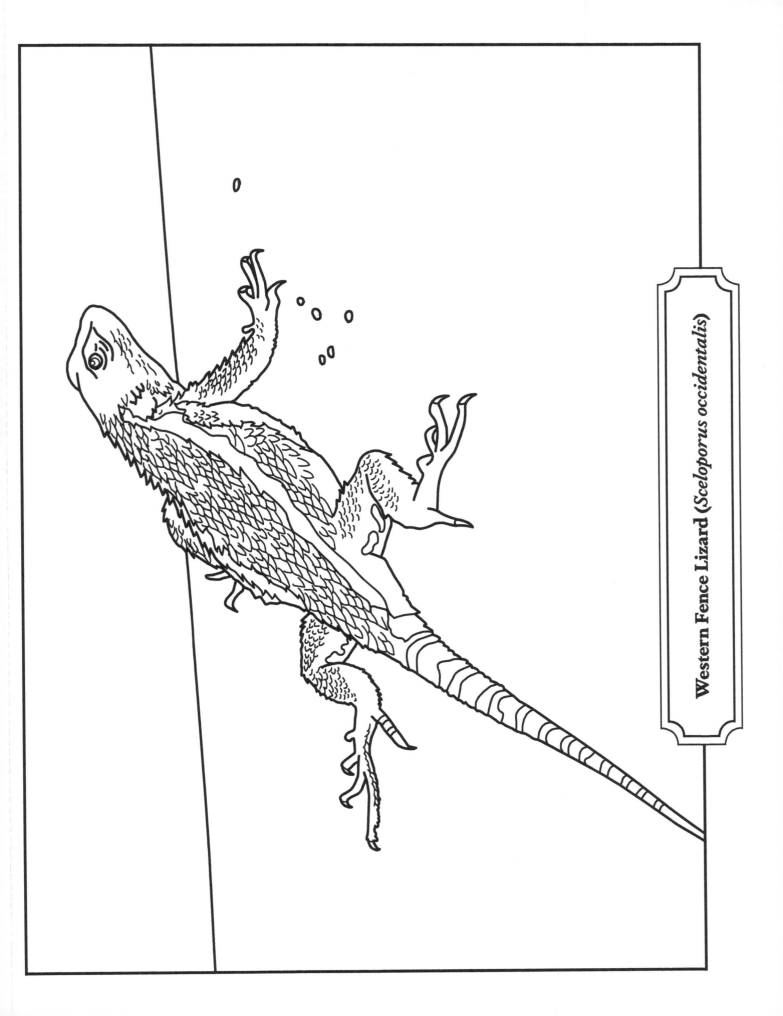

Western Fence Lizard (*Sceloporus occidentalis*)

Western Pond Turtle (*Actinemys marmorata*)

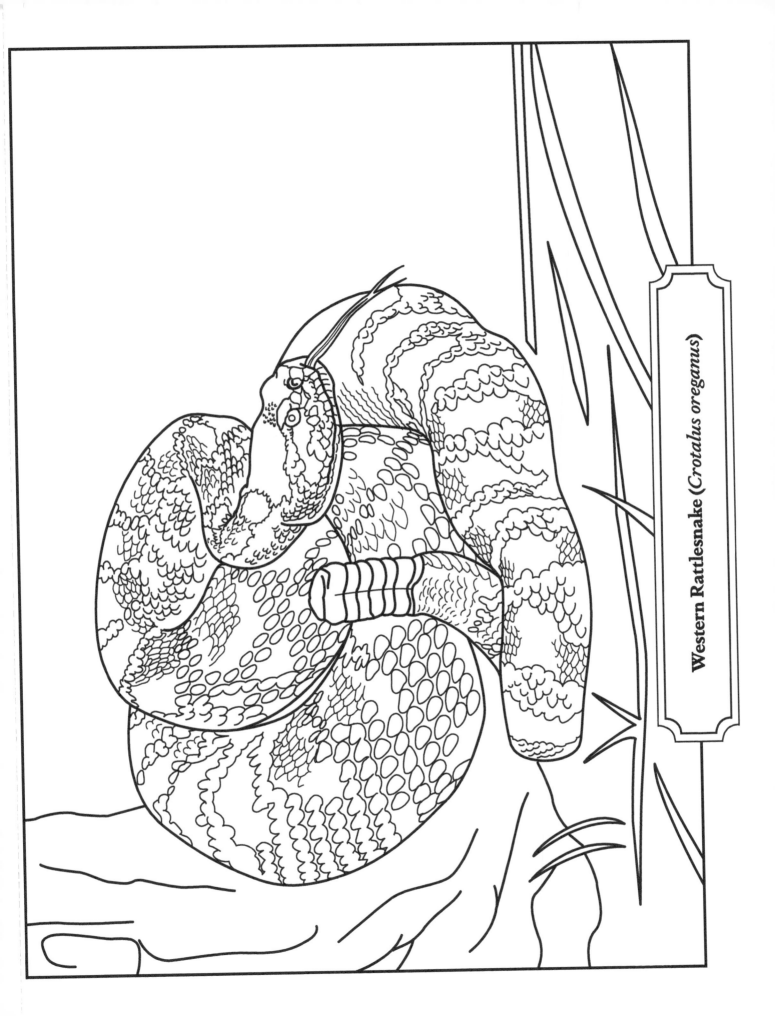

Western Rattlesnake (*Crotalus oreganus*)

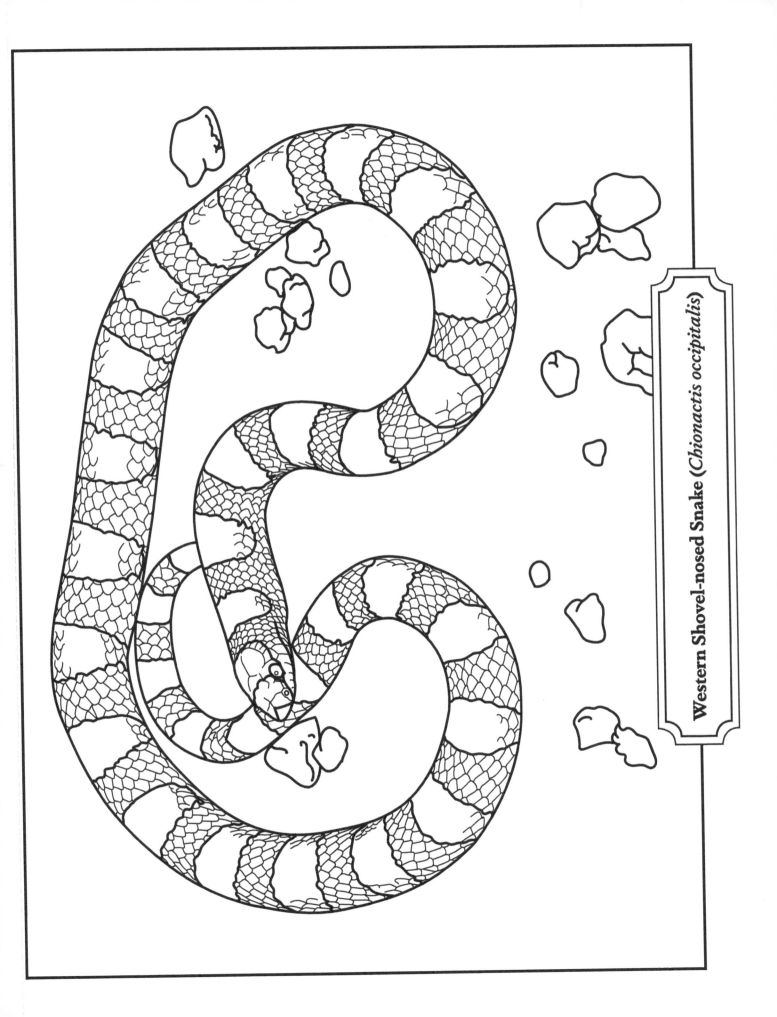

Western Shovel-nosed Snake (*Chionactis occipitalis*)

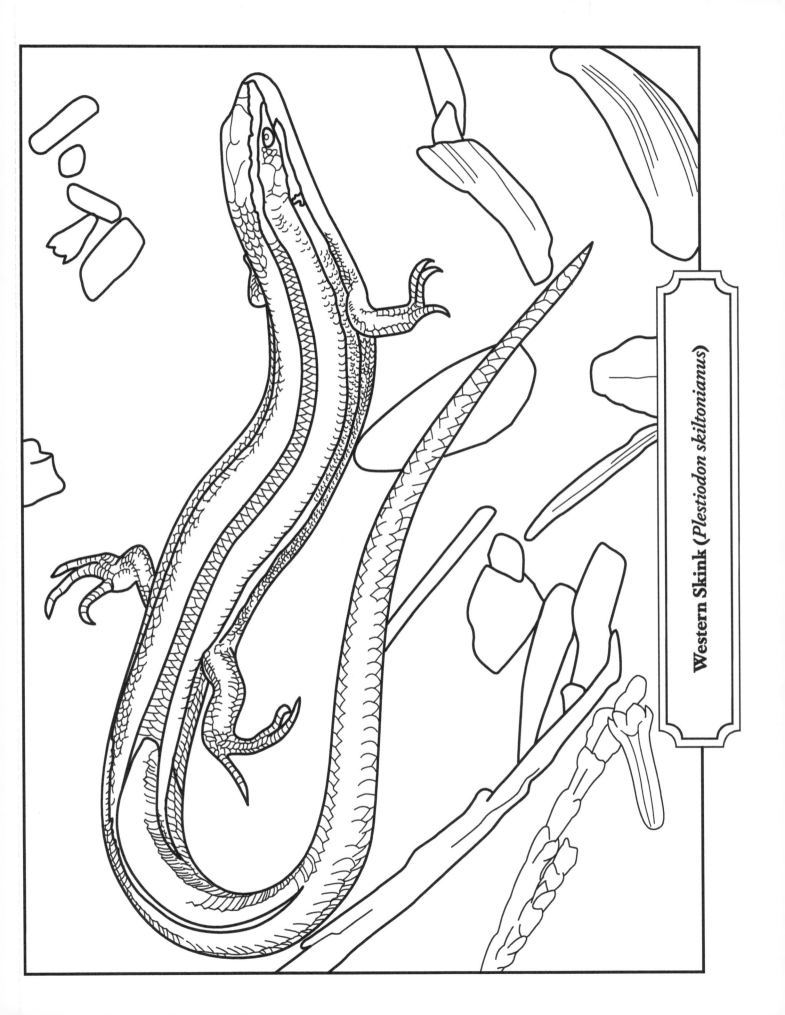

Western Skink (*Plestiodon skiltonianus*)

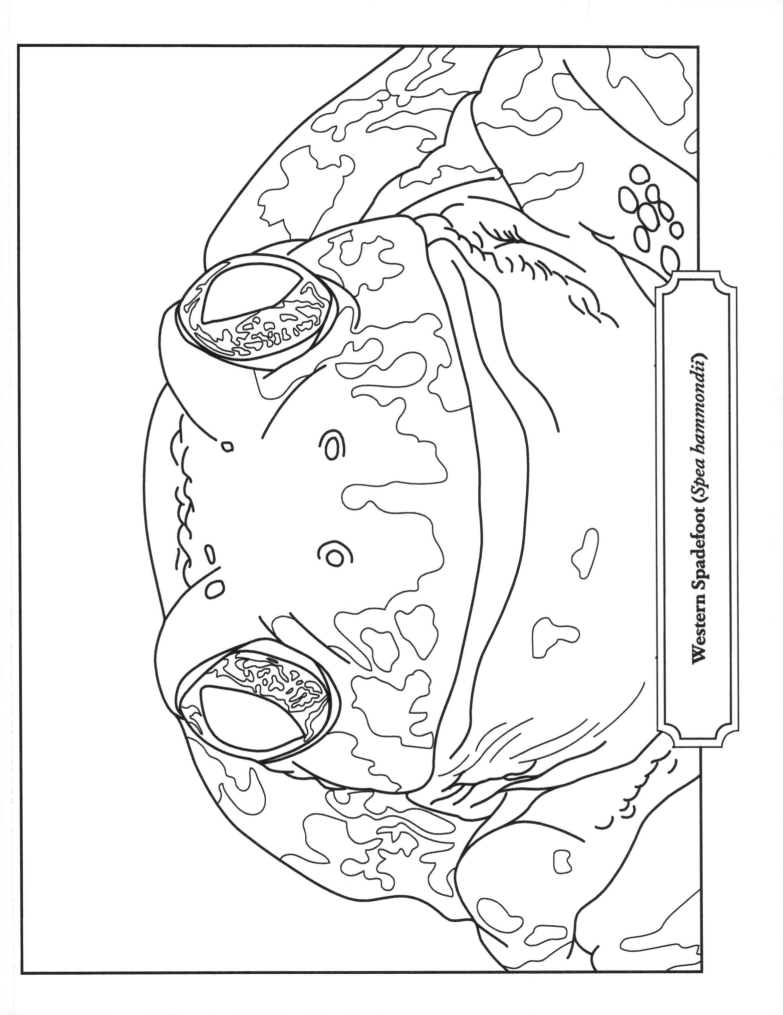

Western Spadefoot (*Spea hammondii*)

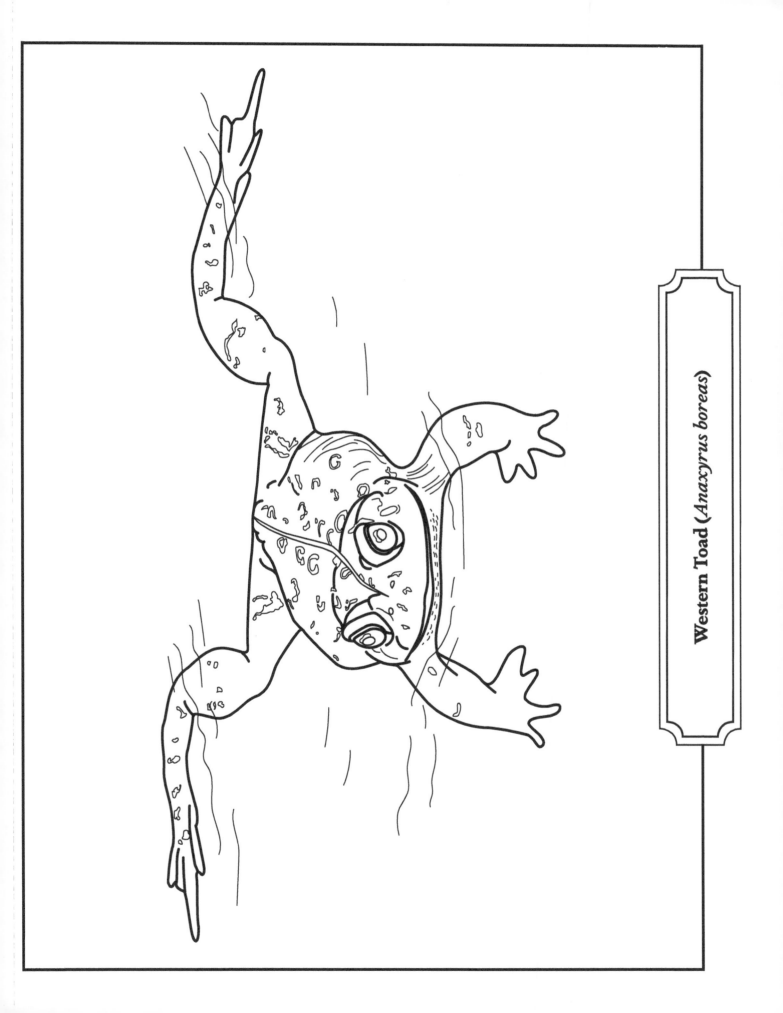

Western Toad (*Anaxyrus boreas*)

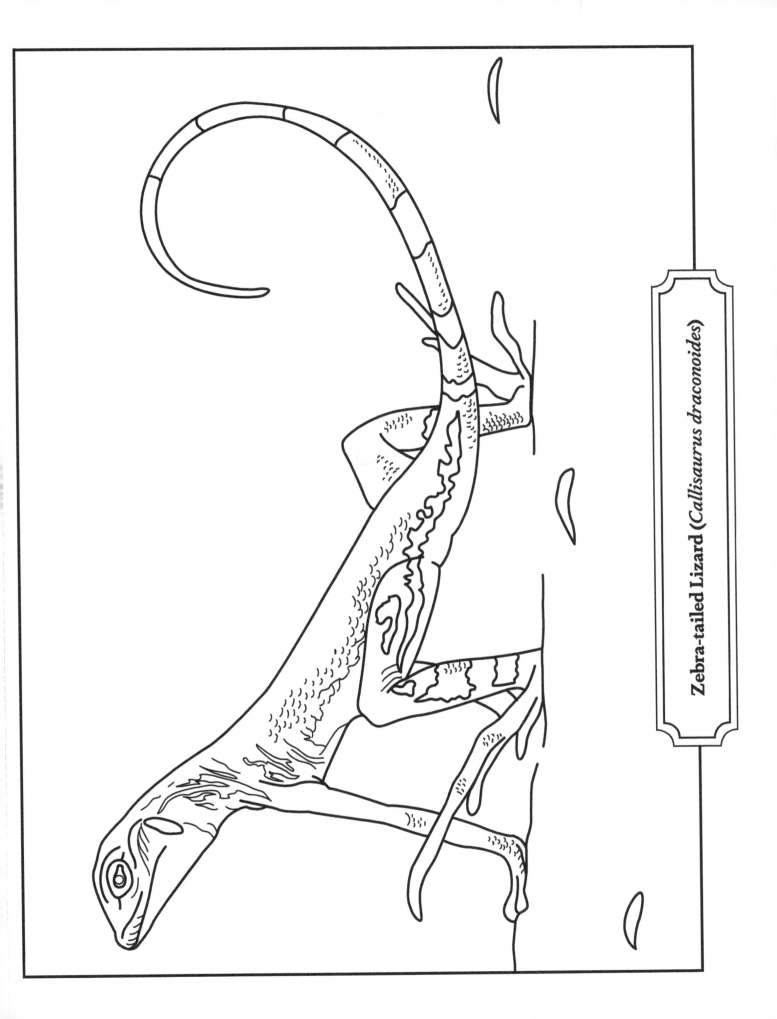

Zebra-tailed Lizard (*Callisaurus draconoides*)

Amphibians and Reptiles

Class (kind), order (type), family / Common Name	Scientific Name	Native	Harmful	Reproductive Mode	Activity	Conservation Status*
Amphibia: Anura: Bufonidae						
Western Toad	Anaxyrus boreas	Native	Poisonous (skin)	Egg-laying	Nocturnal	
Arroyo Toad	Anaxyrus californicus	Native	Poisonous (skin)	Egg-laying	Nocturnal	FE, SSC
Red-spotted Toad	Anaxyrus punctatus	Native	Poisonous (skin)	Egg-laying	Nocturnal	
Amphibia: Anura: Hyliidae						
Pacific Treefrog	Pseudacris regilla	Native	Harmless	Egg-laying	Nocturnal	
Amphibia: Anura: Scaphiopodidae						
Western Spadefoot	Spea hammondii	Native	Harmless	Egg-laying	Nocturnal	SSC
Amphibia: Caudata: Ambystomatidae						
Barred Tiger Salamander	Ambystoma mavortium	Introduced	Harmless	Egg-laying	Nocturnal	
Amphibia: Caudata: Plethodontidae						
Large-blotched Ensatina	Ensatina klauberi	Native	Harmless	Egg-laying	Nocturnal	
Amphibia: Caudata: Salamandridae						
California Newt	Taricha torosa	Native	Poisonous (skin)	Egg-laying	Diurnal or Nocturnal	
Reptilia: Lacertilia: Anguidae						
Southern Alligator Lizard	Elgaria multicarinata	Native	Harmless	Egg-laying	Diurnal	
Reptilia: Lacertilia: Iguanidae						
Desert Iguana	Dipsosaurus dorsalis	Native	Harmless	Egg-laying	Diurnal	
Common Chuckwalla	Sauromalus ater	Native	Harmless	Egg-laying	Diurnal	
Reptilia: Lacertilia: Phrynosomatidae						
Zebra-tailed Lizard	Callisaurus draconoides	Native	Harmless	Egg-laying	Diurnal	
Banded Rock Lizard	Petrosaurus mearnsi	Native	Harmless	Egg-laying	Diurnal	
Blainville's Horned Lizard	Phrynosoma blainvillii	Native	Harmless	Egg-laying	Diurnal	SSC
Flat-tailed Horned Lizard	Phrynosoma mcallii	Native	Harmless	Egg-laying	Diurnal	SSC
Desert Spiny Lizard	Sceloporus magister	Native	Harmless	Egg-laying	Diurnal	
Western Fence Lizard	Sceloporus occidentalis	Native	Harmless	Egg-laying	Diurnal	
Granite Spiny Lizard	Sceloporus orcutti	Native	Harmless	Egg-laying	Diurnal	
Common Side-blotched Lizard	Uta stansburiana	Native	Harmless	Egg-laying	Diurnal	
Reptilia: Lacertilia: Polychrotidae						
Green Anole	Anolis carolinensis	Introduced	Harmless	Egg-laying	Diurnal	

*FE = Federally Endangered, FT = Federally Threatened, SSC = California Species of Special Concern

Class (kind), order (type), family Common Name	Scientific Name	Native	Harmful	Reproductive Mode	Activity	Conservation Status*
Reptilia: Lacertilia: Scincidae						
Western Skink	Plestiodon skiltonianus	Native	Harmless	Egg-laying	Diurnal	
Reptilia: Lacertilia: Teiidae						
Orange-throated Whiptail	Aspidoscelis hyperythrus	Native	Harmless	Egg-laying	Diurnal	
Tiger Whiptail	Aspidoscelis tigris	Native	Harmless	Egg-laying	Diurnal	SSC
Reptilia: Lacertilia: Xantusiidae						
Granite Night Lizard	Xantusia henshawi	Native	Harmless	Live-bearing	Diurnal or Nocturnal	
Reptilia: Serpentes: Boidae						
Rosy Boa	Lichanura trivirgata	Native	Harmless	Live-bearing	Diurnal or Nocturnal	
Reptilia: Serpentes: Colubridae						
Western Shovel-nosed Snake	Chionactis occipitalis	Native	Harmless	Egg-laying	Nocturnal	
Ring-necked Snake	Diadophis punctatus	Native	Harmless	Egg-laying	Nocturnal	SSC
California Kingsnake	Lampropeltis californiae	Native	Harmless	Egg-laying	Diurnal or Nocturnal	
Coast Mountain Kingsnake	Lampropeltis multifasciata	Native	Harmless	Egg-laying	Diurnal or Nocturnal	
Coachwhip	Masticophis flagellum	Native	Harmless	Egg-laying	Diurnal	
Striped Racer	Masticophis lateralis	Native	Harmless	Egg-laying	Diurnal	
Gophersnake	Pituophis catenifer	Native	Harmless	Egg-laying	Diurnal or Nocturnal	
Long-nosed Snake	Rhinocheilus lecontei	Native	Harmless	Egg-laying	Nocturnal	SSC
Two-striped Gartersnake	Thamnophis hammondii	Native	Harmless	Live-bearing	Diurnal or Nocturnal	SSC
Reptilia: Serpentes: Viperidae						
Sidewinder	Crotalus cerastes	Native	Venomous	Live-bearing	Nocturnal	
Western Rattlesnake	Crotalus oreganus	Native	Venomous	Live-bearing	Diurnal or Nocturnal	
Red Diamond Rattlesnake	Crotalus ruber	Native	Venomous	Live-bearing	Diurnal or Nocturnal	SSC
Reptilia: Testudines: Emydidae						
Western Pond Turtle	Actinemys marmorata	Native	Harmless	Egg-laying	Diurnal	SSC
Pond Slider	Trachemys scripta	Introduced	Harmless	Egg-laying	Diurnal	
Reptilia: Testudines: Testudinidae						
Desert Tortoise	Gopherus agassizii	Native	Harmless	Egg-laying	Diurnal	FT, SSC

1) Arroyo Toad (*Anaxyrus californicus*) Body Length: 1.75-3.2 inches

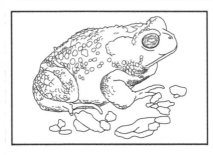

The Arroyo Toad is a small species that specializes in living in sandy arroyo bottoms where it relies on shallow, slow-moving water to breed. Like other toads, it has grandular skin that secretes toxins to ward off predators. The two large glands behind the eyes, called the parotid glands, are lightly colored in front but darker behind. Toad eyes have a horizontal pupil and wildly patterned irises. Active only at night, they spend the day burrowed in sandy soils. At sunset, they emerge on the surface to forage or breed. The male has a "trilling" advertisement call to attract females to the stream's edge. Found from the coast to foothills, the Arroyo Toad is a federally endangered species due to reduced population sizes and their specialized life-history preferences of inhabiting only arroyos.

2) Banded Rock Lizard (*Petrosaurus mearnsi*) Length: 2.6-4.2 inches

The Banded Rock Lizard has tones of gray, brown, orange, and blue and blends with the granitic rock surfaces it prefers to run on. Fine points of white on the lizard's back and legs resemble the sparkle of the quartz embedded in the granite stone. Rarely ever leaving the boulders, it has a flattened body, widely-splayed legs, and strong claws to help it grip to vertical or inverted surfaces. Found strictly in the desert, this species likes to bask in the sunshine on large rock surfaces and granite boulders. It retreats and sleeps in rock cracks. Cunning, wary, and calculated, it is hard to approach and keeps a safe distance by running to the opposite side of the rock, adjusting escape options continuously. Females lay eggs in the mid spring to early summer, which hatch in the late summer.

3) Barred Tiger Salamander (*Ambystoma mavortium*) Length: 3-6.5 inches

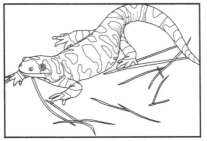

An introduced species to southern California, the Barred Tiger Salamander is isolated to a few freshwater ponds but is expanding its range and colonizing new areas. Native to the central United States, it is unknown how it was released into southern California, but the species has been sold in the pet trade and their smaller larvae are used as bait by fisherman. Boldly patterned, this rotund salamander has a dark gray to black ground color with yellow blotches and bars. The adults use slow-moving freshwater ponds and reservoirs, where they return yearly to breed. Migrations of the Barred Tiger Salamander are nocturnal and commence at the first strong winter rains. Adults can be found walking overland towards their natal ponds returning to the same body of water from where they were born. This species has a complete life-cycle that includes a gilled-larval stage needing to be underwater. Metamorphosis is similar to a frog, and the larval form transforms into an adult who can then leave the pond.

4) Blainville's Horned Lizard (*Phrynosoma blainvillii*) Length: 2.5-4.5 inches

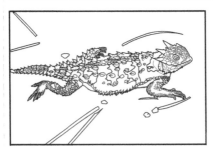

A master of camouflage, the Blainville's Horned Lizard uses its color pattern, scalation, and behavior to blend into the environment. With color tones of a yellow to brown base color, it has larger blotches of dark brown arranged in repeating patterns down its back. Enlarged tubercles and fringe scales create a bumpy body surface and break up the lizard's outline against the sandy or pebbly surfaces it sits on. A crown of horns around the back of the head are actively used to defend the neck from attack. Found from the coast to mountains, this species prefers habitats that are flat and free of grasses. It has a strict diet of harvester ants and a specialized physiology to handle their formic acid chemical defense. Finally, it uses the extreme defensive behavior of squirting blood from the corner of its eye to distract predators such as coyotes and foxes. It is believed the blood contains an aromatic irritant laced with formic acid obtained from their ant diet. Females lay eggs in the late spring to early summer, which hatch in the late summer.

5) California Kingsnake (*Lampropeltis californiae*) — Length: 20-85 inches

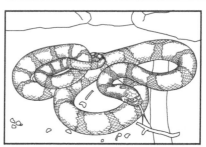

A large, muscular constrictor, the California Kingsnake is usually banded with alternating colors of chocolate brown to black and white to yellowish cream. In some localized regions, the color pattern is polymorphic. A mixture of the traditional banded color pattern can be found along with an all black pattern that has a single mid-dorsal light stripe running down the middle of the back. California Kingsnakes are effective hunters and eat a wide variety of prey items including snakes, rodents, birds and their young, and lizards. This includes eating rattlesnakes. They are thought to be immune to their venom. They are effective climbers and ascend into trees to seek out bird nests. Found from the coast to the deserts, they inhabit a wide-variety of habitats and have readily adapted to urban settings. They are active in both day or night depending on seasonal temperatures. Females lay eggs in the late spring to early summer, which hatch in the late summer.

6) California Newt (*Taricha torosa*) — Length: 2.75-3.5 inches

The California Newt is brown above and orange below. Its glandular skin produces extremely strong toxins that deter anything from eating them. When harassed, it bends it back and lifts its legs to show off its bright orange belly and undersides. Milky white secretions contain powerful neurotoxins that protects them from being eaten. Found in coastal and foothill streams, this species has a complete life-cycle with a fully aquatic gilled larval stage that requires metamorphosis to complete the development to the adult form. Every year, adults migrate back to the streams after the first winter rains. Once in the water, the body transforms for an aquatic life. The tail, used for swimming, grows higher and more paddle-like. The skin thins and its glandular texture disappears allowing them to breath underwater. After breeding, the adults leave the water to find hiding places to wait out the hot dry summer months.

7) Coachwhip (*Masticophis flagellum*) — Length: 24-102 inches

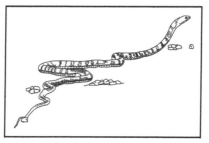

One of the longest snakes in the region, the Coachwhip is impressive for its size and speed. It has an enlarged, pointed head with large eyes. Its neck has distinctive black markings forming offset diagonal crossbars. Sometimes called the "Red Racer," its body can be colored salmon red, but the species is polymorphic and additional body colors exist ranging from black to yellow. Strictly diurnal, Coachwhips hunt lizards by actively chasing them down. The hunt is aggressive, fast, and without mercy. Prey is swallowed immediately after capture while still alive. It also eats mammals, snakes, frogs, small turtles, insects, and carrion. Found in either coastal or desert habitats, this species prefers open areas where whiptails are abundant. Females lay eggs in the late spring to early summer, which hatch in the late summer.

8) Coast Mountain Kingsnake (*Lampropeltis multifasciata*) — Length: 20-48 inches

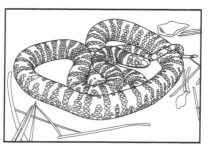

A beautiful, elegant snake with slender proportions, the Coast Mountain Kingsnake is the most vibrantly-colored snake in the region with red, black, and white cross-bands. The tri-colored markings mimic those of coral snakes and deter predation by birds and possibly other types of predators. The mimicry is interesting because the region has no coral snakes to reinforce the predator deterrence. A constrictor, it preys on lizards, snakes, birds and their eggs, and small mammals. Found from the coast to mountains, it can be found in milder climates of coniferous forests, oak woodlands, and riparian corridors. They are active in either the day or night depending on seasonal temperatures and frequent parts of the forests that have fallen logs or rock outcrops. Females lay eggs in the late spring to early summer, which hatch in the late summer.

9) Common Chuckwalla (*Sauromalus ater*)   Length: 5-9 inches

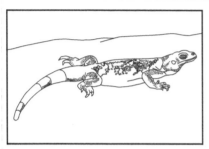

One of the region's largest lizards, the chuckwalla is a type of iguana that lives in rocky habitats restricted to deserts. It has a light brown or tan ground color. Adult males become melanistic to varying degrees, usually with black on their heads, chest, and pelvis. Some have orange or red on their mid-body. The tail is banded with alternating light brown and dark gray colors. Found basking on rocks throughout the region's deserts, the chuckwalla is a specialists at using rock crevices for sleeping and retreats. If a predator attempts to pull them from the crevice, they inflate their lungs to wedge the body in place. A strict herbivore, individuals often climb into nearby shrubs to forage on flowers, leaves, and stems. Females lay eggs in the mid spring and early summer, which hatch in the late summer.

10) Common Side-blotched Lizard (*Uta stansburiana*)   Length: 1.5-2.5 inches

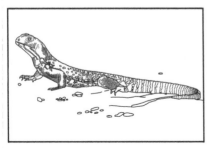

The small, but readily seen Common Side-blotched Lizard, is generally light tan to brown. Under closer inspection, adult males are spectacular in coloration with light turquoise blue marks and speckles with an infusion of yellow and orange. Their black slide-blotch is located behind their forelegs and is used in territorial display. Underneath, the belly is white but the throat is colored with yellow, orange, or blue. Each throat coloration corresponds to different reproductive strategies, with blue throat morphs being the most aggressive and yellow throat morphs being the least aggressive. Found from the coast to the deserts, this species is a ground dweller and perches on small rocks or sticks. Active in the day, it basks in the sun to thermoregulate. Females lay eggs in the late spring to early summer, which hatch in the late summer.

11) Desert Iguana (*Dipsosaurus dorsalis*)   Length: 4-5.75 inches

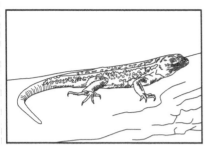

A hardy desert inhabitant, the Desert Iguana is white and gray in coloration, often with an infusion of rusty red streaks along its neck and sides. Iguanas bask in the open and can be seen perched on small rocks or mounds. An herbivore, it prefers to eat yellow flowers, but as choices dry up, it will eat leaves and stems. Sometimes it will climb into the desert plants to forage high up in the branches. Found strictly in the desert, this diurnal species has a high tolerance for heat and prefers to keep its body temperature above 104˚F. To escape predation, it uses its speed as a first defense, often running bipedally on its hindlegs to flee for the cover of a bush or diving into an open hole. Females lay eggs in the mid spring to early summer, which hatch in the late summer.

12) Desert Spiny Lizard (*Sceloporus magister*)   Length: 3.25-5.7 inches

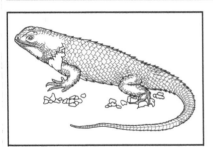

Tougher than most, the Desert Spiny Lizard is a brute. Its stocky build, thick proportions, and strong legs go well with its aggressive attitude and fierce disposition. Its ground color usually consists of grays and browns above. Males are more brightly colored, with scales colored blue and yellow, a prominent black collar on the sides and bottom of its neck, and a light blue throat. Underneath, bright blue belly patches are infused with iridescent green. Males show off the blue belly by standing high on their legs and doing push-ups. Each scale is pointed giving its body a rough appearance and strong armament. Found strictly in the desert, this species lives in a variety of habitats but prefers thick vegetation with large branches to perch on. Basking allows them to thermoregulate, keep a lookout for potential intruders or rivals, and seek out mates. Wary, it is calculating, and runs into the densest thickets to escape from predators. Females lay eggs in the mid spring to early summer, which hatch in the late summer.

13) Desert Tortoise (*Gopherus agassizii*) — Length: 6-15 inches

The Desert Tortoise has an oval-domed shell with thick scutes to serve as an effective armament. The shell has yellowish-brown scutes bordered by darker browns or blacks, while other body parts are uniformly light brown in coloration. The front legs are heavily scaled and used as protective covers when the head is fully retracted into their shell. A fully terrestrial species, tortoises use their beak to bite into thicker plants like cacti, but prefer eating flowers if available. Active in the daytime, the Desert Tortoise is unable to tolerate the hottest parts of the day and retreats into deeply-dug burrows. Found strictly in the desert, this species inhabits regions with stable soils for digging burrows. It mostly inhabits flat areas with plentiful vegetation, but it can also scale rocky hillsides. Females lay up to 12 eggs in the late spring to early summer, which hatch in the late summer.

14) Flat-tailed Horned Lizard (*Phrynosoma mcallii*) — Length: 2.5-3.25 inches

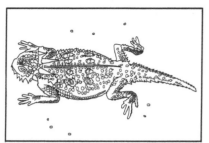

More than most horned lizards, the Flat-tailed Horned Lizard is a master of camouflage. Using its color pattern, scalation, and behavior, it blends with sandy and rocky surfaces. Beige, yellow, and light browns, offset by white highlights, make up its ground color. Its body has fewer enlarged tubercles and finer scalation in perfect proportion to the sand to pebble ratio of soils it lives on. Dark brown blotches and a mid-dorsal line pattern the back. This species has a longer than average tail for horned lizards, flattened at its base, and colored with yellow-orange and white. Rather than speeding away when approached, it stays hunkered down and relies on crypsis—its abililty to conceal itself by blending into its surrounding environment. Found in flat open deserts, this species inhabits sand dunes, sand flats, desert pavement, and mudstone badlands. It has a strict diet of harvester ants and a specialized physiology to handle their formic acid defenses. Finally, it uses the extreme defensive behavior of squirting aromatic acid-laden blood from the corner of its eye to distract predators such as coyotes and foxes. Females lay eggs in spring, which hatch in the early summer.

15) Gophersnake (*Pituophis catenifer*) — Length: 30-110 inches

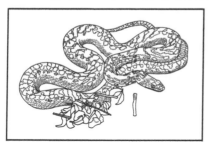

The Gophersnake is one of the region's more common snakes in and around urbanized areas. One of the largest snakes in our region, this constrictor has a muscular body colored with brown and yellow markings. Black blotches extend down the length of the back. The eye is usually orange. Its large body is used to constrict prey as big as a rabbit. They also eat other mammals and sometimes birds, their eggs, and lizards. When approached, they hiss loudly and flatten their head into a triangular shape. In addition, they vibrate their tail, which mimics that of a rattlesnake. Found from the coast to the deserts, this species lives in a variety of habitats. It is active in either the day or night, depending on seasonal temperatures. Females lay eggs in the late spring to early summer, which hatch in the late summer or early fall.

16) Granite Night Lizard (*Xantusia henshawi*) — Length: 2-2.8 inches

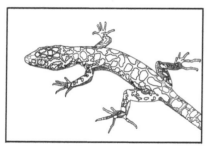

Granite Night Lizards are small and secretive. Specialized for living in granitic rock cracks, they have flattened bodies and widely-splayed legs. Wide, scale plates cover the head, while the body has fine granular scales to allow for great flexibility. Blotches are dark gray separated by a network of reticulated interspaces of light gray infused with lines of yellow. The tail is easily broken off and serves as an anti-predator adaptation. Like most lizards, the tail can be regenerated and the new tail regrows after a period of a few months. Found from the inland foothills to the desert slopes, this species is restricted to the types of granitic rock that readily flakes. Flaking creates narrow rock crevices in which the lizard lives the majority of its life. Unlike most lizards, females only produce one or two offspring a year and do not lay eggs. Instead, they gestate their young internally and babies are born live as miniatures of the adults.

17) Granite Spiny Lizard (*Sceloporus orcutti*) Length: 3.25-4.6 inches

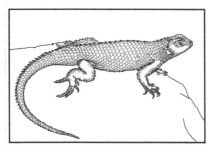

A robust lizard, the Granite Spiny Lizard has wide, pointed scales that serve as an effective armament. Juveniles and females are brown with darker brown crossbars, but adult males become vibrant blue-green with a broad purple stripe down the middle of their backs. Underneath, bright blue belly patches are infused with iridescent green. To defend territories from rivals and impress females, males show off their blue belly markings by standing high on their legs and doing push-ups. Found from the coast to the desert, this species lives on granite boulders. From their rocky perches, they bask in the sun to thermoregulate. Wary, they quickly flee when anyone approaches, even from great distances. Females lay eggs in the late spring to early summer, which hatch in the late summer.

18) Green Anole (*Anolis carolinensis*) Length: 2-5.3 inches

An introduced species to urban parks, the Green Anole is native to the southeastern United States. This small lizard has a high ridged back and long pointed snout. A master at color change, anoles are able to go from brown to green in seconds. When active, the body is lime green with a straight or zig-zag mid-dorsal light brown stripe running down the middle of the back. Underneath the body is white. The eye has a suffusion of blue on its eyelids. Males display to potential rivals and females by stretching out their dewlap, a flat semi-circular throat display that is colored peach-orange to red. Found in thick, leafy vegetation in isolated introduced populations, this species likes to bask on tree trunks, broad leaves, stems, and branches. Rarely found on the ground, it is consider a mid-height arboreal species. Females lay eggs in the late spring to early summer, which hatch in the late summer.

19) Large-blotched Ensatina (*Ensatina klauberi*) Length: 1.5-3 inches

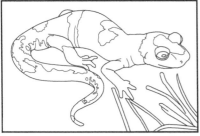

Boldly patterned with yellow to orange blotches on a dark gray to black body, the Large-blotched Ensatina uses its striking color pattern to warn potential predators that it has toxic skin. When harassed, it secretes a milky white poison onto its skin which has little effect on people but likely is a strong deterrent to a coyote or fox. Found in the oak and pine forests of the foothills and mountains, this nocturnal salamander spends the majority of its life in subterranean hide-outs. During winter rains it emerges at night to forage and look for mates. Ensatinas lack a free-living larval stage. Instead, they have direct developing eggs that can be laid on land allowing them to live farther away from bodies of water. Eggs are laid in moist environments beneath rocks or fallen logs and hatch as miniatures of the adult form requiring no metamorphosis.

20) Long-nosed Snake (*Rhinocheilus lecontei*) Length: 19-60 inches

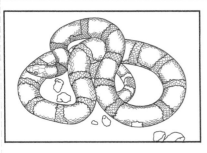

The Long-nosed Snake has a mild, slender build and an imperfect tri-colored pattern mimicking the coral snake. Its broad black saddles are speckled with cream white, while the narrower interspaces are cream white infused with orangish-red. It has a long snout, narrow head, and little indication of a neck. Smaller meals, like lizards and their eggs, are swallowed directly, while larger prey items are constricted. Active at night, it hunts other snakes, mammals, and birds. Often confused for a kingsnake, some localized populations lack orange or red colors, resulting in a body pattern of black and white bands. Found in both coastal and desert habitats, this species likes loose-soils and is a good burrower. Females lay eggs in the late spring to early summer, which hatch in the late summer or early fall.

21) Orange-throated Whiptail (*Aspidoscelis hyperythrus*) — Length: 2-2.75 inches

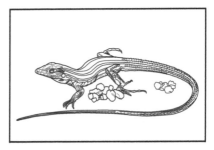

Fast and active, the Orange-throated Whiptail is a slender lizard with a pointed snout and long, thin tail. Brown above, this species has light brown to white stripes running the length of the back. Adult males seasonally acquire their bright orange throat coloration that sometimes extends to the chest and underside of the tail. The orange pigment is derived from carotenoids and is acquired from their arthropod diet. Whiptails are active foragers that are constantly sniffing through leaf-litter for a meal. Periodically, they'll stop in a warm spot and press their belly against the ground to thermoregulate. Found only in coastal habitats, this species prefers sagebrush habitats with open flat soils. Females lay eggs in the late spring to early summer, which hatch in the late summer.

22) Pacific Treefrog (*Pseudacris regilla*) — Length: 0.75-2 inches

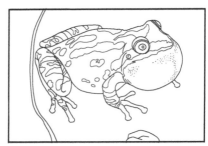

The Pacific Treefrog is a small delicate frog with smooth thin skin. The body can be colored light gray, brown, or green with dark brown to black blotches. With long hindlegs, it is an able jumper. Its toes have an expanded tip that aid in climbing, although it never truly climbs trees. Instead, they prefer to be near aquatic vegetation like rushes and reeds. Found in a wide-variety of aquatic habitats from the coast to the desert, the Pacific Treefrog is one of our more common frogs. It is active only at night. The male has a two-part "ribbit" advertisement call and seasonally set up a breeding territory to call from. Their vocal sac is usually colored light green and is used to amplify the call. The male's vocal slits are located on the floor of the mouth and the "ribbit" sound is made as he pushes air back and forth between his lungs and vocal sac.

23) Pond Slider (*Trachemys scripta*) — Length: 3.5-14.5 inches

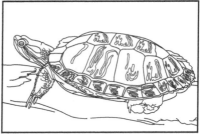

An introduced species from the pet trade, the Pond Slider is a prominent inhabitant to reserviors, streams, and ponds. The shell is domed with green, yellow, and black concentric markings. The head and neck are lined with greens and yellows. A large red blotch is located behind each eye giving this turtle the alternative name of the "Red-eared Slider." With broad webbed hindfeet, it is a powerful swimmer. Its front feet contain long sharp claws used to tear apart food items. It eats plants, fish, tadpoles, crayfish, snails, and insects. It is found in coastal regions where it has been introduced into manmade ponds and reservoirs, but it readily travels overland to colonize additional streams and ponds. It is known to displace the native Western Pond Turtle. Females lay up to 60 eggs in the late spring to early summer, which hatch in the late summer or early fall.

24) Red Diamond Rattlesnake (*Crotalus ruber*) — Length: 29-65 inches

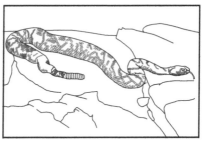

The region's largest rattlesnake, the Red Diamond is a heavy-bodied terrestrial species. Colored with brick red to orange, the body generally lacks black speckles or marks. The diamond-shaped blotches extend the length of the body and are highlighted with white. The triangular head is large and uniformly colored except for a wide preocular stripe in front of the eye and a more narrow postocular stripe behind the eye. The "raccoon" tail has alternating black and white bands immediately before the rattle. It hunts by ambush and eats squirrels, rabbits, rats, birds, and lizards. Generally shy and secretive, it requires more serious threats to become defensive and rattle. Found from the coast to the desert slopes, it inhabits a wide variety of habitats. Females give live birth to as many as 20 young in the mid summer months.

25) Red-spotted Toad (*Anaxyrus punctatus*) — Length: 1.5-3 inches

The Red-spotted Toad has a pointed snout and round parotid glands. True to their name, the glandular skin has red spots on a light gray to olive background. In less frequent cases, some individuals have no red-spots and are uniform in coloration. Found only in the desert at the bottom of mountain stream drainages, this toad relies on strong late winter to early spring rains to bring water to the desert floor. The male uses a "trilling" advertisement call to attract females back to the water who usually forage a mile or more away. The call is amplified in the male's vocal sac and can be heard from great distances. Females lay thousands of eggs which quickly hatch into tadpoles. After foraging on algae for a period of a few weeks, the tadpoles go through metamorphosis. The tail is absorbed, legs are grown, lungs and eyelids develop, and after the dramatic transformation is complete, the small toadlet is ready to leave the water.

26) Ring-necked Snake (*Diadophis punctatus*) — Length: 8-34 inches

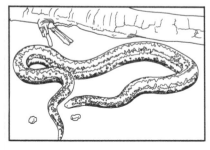

The Ring-necked Snake has a small, slender body uniformly colored with olive green. Its head is dark gray to black, with a distinctive orange or yellow narrow ring around its neck. Underneath, the body is brightly colored with orange and red, which intensifies to bright red on the undersurfaces of the tail. When threatened, it coils its tail into a flattened plate and inverts it upward. How the display is effective is still unknown. Bright colorations are known to serve as deterrents to predators signaling an animal is either poisonous or venomous. While the Ring-neck Snake likely has mild venom to small prey, the toxicity would likely be harmless to a larger predator. Or, the tail display could serve as a diversion from the head to focus an attack to non-critical areas of the body. Found from the coast to mountains, this species prefers moist habitats including riparian corridors, oak woodlands, and coniferous forests. Active at night, it hunts slender salamanders, frogs, and other snakes. Females lay eggs in the late spring to early summer, which hatch in the late summer.

27) Rosy Boa (*Lichanura trivirgata*) — Length: 17-44 inches

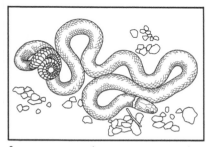

A muscular constrictor, the Rosy Boa has smooth small scales that gives the body an elegant sleek skin. Generally colored in shades of gray, their pattern is highly variable across their range. Some individuals are uniform light gray with dark gray speckles, while others have rosy peach stripes. Stripes can be finely delineated with straight edges or highly irregular with undulating indented margins. Its small eye is usually orange. Known for its docile demeanor, the Rosy Boa hunts for rodents and other small animals at night and uses constriction to subdue its prey. Found from the coast to the desert, it lives in rocky terrain. It is a long-lived species that never travels far from its retreats or hunting grounds. Females give live birth to up to 14 young that are born as smaller versions of the adult form.

28) Sidewinder (*Crotalus cerastes*) — Length: 17-33 inches

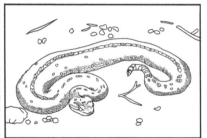

A type of rattlesnake, the Sidewinder is best known for its unusual sideways undulating locomotion. Like other rattlesnakes, it is an ambush hunter that relies heavily on camouflage to conceal its location. Generally light brown or sand tan above, its blotches extending down the middle of the back are darker brown to butterscotch in color. Small black blotches or speckles punctuate the sides. The head is triangular in shape due to the enlarged venom glands housed in the back of the head. The eye is concealed by a prominent post-ocular stripe, while the eye itself is cryptically colored to blend in with the head coloration. The rattle is small and colored light brown. It eats kangaroo rats, mice, and lizards. Found strictly in the desert, it prefers flat terrain with either windblown sands or fine pebble rocks. Active primarily at night, it will extend its ambush time by staying coiled into the early morning hours after sunrise. Females give live birth to more than 15 young in the late spring to mid summer.

29) Southern Alligator Lizard (*Elgaria multicarinata*)   Length: 2.9-7 inches

The fierce Southern Alligator Lizard has a light tan to dark gray body with darker crossbars containing white highlights. The eye is orange to red with a black pupil. It has a wide-array of defensive strategies to protect itself from being eaten. If confronted by a predator, this lizard will first stand its ground and display an open mouth. If grabbed it will actively bite back and twist its body. And like other lizards, it has the ability to drop its tail, leaving it to wiggle and twist to distract the predator as it runs off and hides. Found in a wide-variety of habitats from the coast to the mountains, the Southern Alligator Lizard likes places with lots of cover, including fallen logs, rock piles, and areas with plenty of leaf-litter. Active in the day-time from spring to fall, this species is often seen around gardens and homes. Females lay eggs in the late spring to early summer, which hatch in the late summer.

30) Striped Racer (*Masticophis lateralis*)   Length: 22-60 inches

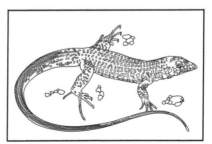

The Striped Racer, with its slender, agile frame, has a dark brown to black head and body with two cream-white lateral stripes extending down the sides of the body from the head to the tail. Its head has white spots on the sides of the snout and around their large eyes. Its belly is usually white to yellow transitioning to coral pink underneath the tail. It is strictly diurnal and hunts with its head elevated above the ground. During a hunt, it is fast and aggressive, outpacing the fastest lizards. It is also known to eat other snakes, frogs, small mammals, birds, and insects. Found primarily in coastal chaparral habitats, it is also found in the mountains among coniferous trees. One of the region's more common snakes, the Striped Racer is seen in natural habitats bordering urbanized areas. It is often observed basking on flat rocks or in the middle of hiking trails, but is easily startled and slithers away at high speeds. Females lay eggs in the late spring to early summer, which hatch in the late summer.

31) Tiger Whiptail (*Aspidoscelis tigris*)   Length: 2.4-5 inches

Fast and active, the Tiger Whiptail is a medium-sized lizard with a pointed snout and long tail. Its body is brown with lighter markings. Striped as juveniles, the color pattern transforms as they develop into adults and becomes a complicated mix of bars and stripes often resulting in broken marks. Whiptails are active foragers who are constantly on the move. They sniff through leaf-litter for a meal, patrolling great distances in a single day. Periodically, they'll stop to thermoregulate by finding a warm spot to press their belly against the ground. Sometimes they wiggle down onto the ground to maximize the transfer of heat into their bodies. Found from the coast to the desert, the Tiger Whiptail is a ground dweller that prefers rocky terrain whether in the flats or on steep slopes. Females lay eggs in the late spring to early summer, which hatch in the late summer.

32) Two-striped Gartersnake (*Thamnophis hammondii*)   Length: 15-40 inches

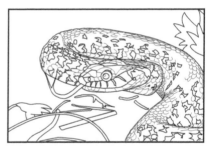

A semi-aquatic species, the Two-striped Gartersnake is olive green above with two lateral light-yellow stripes running down either side. Small black blotches punctuate the body pattern along the side. The head is olive green above and yellowish white below. Labial scales along its large mouth have black stripes separating each scale. The eye is large and its olive-green iris blends in with the head coloration. The tongue is pink to red with a black-forked type and is used for smelling. When the tongue is retracted, scent markers sampled from the air are deposited onto a sensory organ on the roof of the mouth. Regularly swimming on top and below the water, it preys on frogs and tadpoles, fish, fish eggs, and earthworms. It is found from the coast to the desert in a variety of aquatic and semi-aquatic habitats, including streams, ponds, mountain meadows, and vernal pools. Females give live birth to more than 30 young in the late spring to mid summer.

A common lizard in both urban and natural settings, the Western Fence Lizard is brown above with protective pointed scales. In males, the belly has side-by-side blue patches that are bright and vibrant. Males show off the bright blue coloration by standing high on their legs and doing push-ups. Active in the day, this species basks in the open to thermoregulate and look over their territories. This species can change color from brown to nearly black, which allows it to absorb the sun's heat more effectively. Like most lizards, the tail is easily separated from the body and wiggles to distract a predator while they make their escape. After a few months, the tail regrows to a near-replicate of the original. Found from the coast to the mountains, this species prefers to live on fallen logs, tree trunks, and nearby rocks. Around houses and ranches, it can be readily seen on fence posts and wood piles. Females lay eggs in the late spring to early summer, which hatch in the late summer.

The only freshwater turtle native to the region, the Western Pond Turtle is a fully aquatic species. The shell is a flattened oval with olive green to dark brown colors. Black lines and blotches radiate from the center of each scute of the shell. The head and neck have a network of darker reticulations. The beak is lighter and the eye is yellow to orange. It often pulls itself from the water to bask on logs and rocks, usually in spots with deeper water to allow for escape. It eats both plants and a wide variety of aquatic prey including insects, worms, fish, frog eggs, tadpoles, and crayfish. Found in freshwater habitats from the coast to foothills, this species prefers less disturbed ponds, lakes, and streams. Often it is displaced by introduced turtles released by reckless pet owners. Females lay eggs in the late spring to early summer, which hatch in the late summer or early fall.

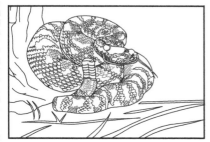

One of the more common snakes in the region, the Western Rattlesnake has a heavy body and prominent triangular head. Colored mainly with browns, individuals can be olive green to black. Dark, regularly-spaced blotches extend down the back, each bordered by a narrow fringe of black. The eye is concealed by a dark brown postocular stripe, while the eye itself is uniformly dark. Among its sensory organs, it uses both its forked tongue and heat-detecting pits to track prey. An ambush hunter, it eats rabbits, rodents, birds, lizards, and sometimes other snakes. Venoms are powerful and contain toxins targeting the destruction of a wide array of molecules in the prey's body. When threatend, the snake will recoil, elevate its head, and vibrate its rattle. The rattle is a series of interlocking shed scales that rub together to produce the sound. It rattles only when fearful for its life, otherwise the rattle is kept hidden when coiled for ambush. Found from the coast to the mountains, the Western Rattlesnake is active either in the day or night depending on seasonal temperatures. Females give live birth to more than 20 young in the late spring to mid summer.

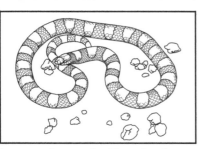

A small, banded snake, the Western Shovel-nosed Snake is a sand burrower that spends a good portion of its life underneath the surface. Its shovel-like snout helps it slip through the sand effortlessly. Its body has repeating dark brown to black saddles that extend the length of the body. The intervening spaces between the saddles are cream white to light yellow. In some, the interspaces include bright orange bands. It moves quickly with tight undulations and the banded pattern makes forward motion difficult to detect. This illusion and the ability to dive beneath the sand without hesitation allows them to escape from predators. Found strictly in the desert, this species prefers flat sandy terrain. They emerge on the surface at night to hunt arthropods. Females lay eggs in the mid spring to early summer, which hatch in the late summer.

37) Western Skink (*Plestiodon skiltonianus*)

Length: 2.1-3.4 inches

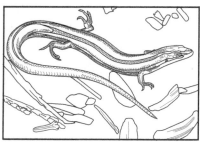

A slender, secretive lizard, the Western Skink has smooth, curved scales that create a shiny sleek armament. The body is brown with light-brown stripes running the length of the back. In juveniles, the tail is neon blue making it readily seen. If attacked, a predator would target the bright blue tail rather than the body, neck, or head. Like most lizards, the tail is easily separated from the body and wiggles to distract a predator while they make their escape. The tail will eventually regrow to be a near-replicate of the original. Adults lose their bright tail coloration, which becomes a dull purple. Found from the coast to the mountains, this species specializes in living close to the ground in dense cover, such as grasses and leaf-litter. With disproportionately small legs, it uses serpentine locomotion to make its way through the microcosm of stalks, leaves, and loose soils. Females lay eggs in the late spring to early summer, which hatch in the late summer.

38) Western Spadefoot (*Spea hammondii*)

Length: 1.5-2.5 inches

The Western Spadefoot is a toad-like frog not related to the true toads, but shares a terrestrial body form due to similar life-history strategies. Similar to a toad, it has short, robust hindlegs used for digging. On the heel of each, is a hard, keratinized spade that resembles a toenail. The hardened spade aids in digging. With vertical pupils, it can be easily distinguished from a toad, whose pupils are horizontal. It also lacks the distinctive parotid glands of true toads and has mildly glandular skin. Usually dark to olive green above, the body has lighter green reticulations. Found mainly in coastal and foothill habitats, this frog likes to breed in slow moving streams or still ponds, including vernal pools found on coastal mesas. It is active only at night. Males make a "snoring" advertisement call to attract females to the pond's edge.

39) Western Toad (*Anaxyrus boreas*)

Length: 2-5 inches

The Western Toad is a robust, hardy animal, with glandular skin that secretes poisons if attacked by a predator. The characteristic mid-dorsal stripe is usually light-cream colored and runs down the middle of the back. The body coloration ranges from green to brown with darker blotches, which helps it blend into its background. The female is larger because she produces large quantities of eggs. Unlike most frogs, the male Western Toad lacks an advertisement call and comes to the water's edge in large aggregations. Active only at night, this common toad is found in a large array of aquatic freshwater habitats including streams, ponds, and lakes. It will travel great distances away from water during the non-breeding season. Found from the coast to the mountains, it has also colonized man-made ponds and agricultural canals in the desert.

40) Zebra-tailed Lizard (*Callisaurus draconoides*)

Length: 2.5-4 inches

A desert speedster, the Zebra-tailed Lizard is one of the fastest lizards on the planet. Its delicate body and long legs allow it to maneuver with great agility even at top speed. Colored with white, light grays, and tan markings above, it effectively blends into the substrate. Males have bright colors of orange, yellow, blue, and black on the sides of the belly, which are shown off to a rival or female by elevating its body high off the ground. Found strictly in the desert, this species specializes in open, flat, sandy terrain where it can use its speed to escape. In addition to its bright belly colors, it arches it tail above its body in dramatic displays to reveal the black bars on the underside. Tail waving is used to distract the predator who may be giving chase and is used in courtship and territorial displays. Females lay eggs in the mid spring to early summer, which hatch in the late summer.